The If Odyssey

Also available from Bloomsbury

The If Machine, Peter Worley

Philosophy for Children Through the Secondary Curriculum, Lizzy Lewis and Nick Chandley

Think Again, John L. Taylor

Why Think?, Sara Stanley

The If Odyssey

A Philosophical Journey Through Greek Myth and Storytelling for 8–16-Year-Olds

Peter Worley

Illustrated by Tamar Levi

BLOOMSBURY

LONDON • NEW DELHI • NEW YORK • SYDNEY

A companion website to accompany this book is available online at:
http://education.worley2.continuumbooks.com

Please type in the URL above to receive your unique password for access to the book's online resources.

If you experience any problems accessing the resources, please contact Continuum at: info@continuumbooks.com

First published 2012 by **A & C Black**
an imprint of Bloomsbury Publishing Plc
50 Bedford Square, London WC1B 3DP
175 Fifth Avenue, New York, NY 10010

www.bloomsbury.com

British Library Cataloguing-in-Publication Data
A catalogue record for this book is available from the British Library.

ISBN: 978-1-4411-7495-6 (paperback)
    978-1-4411-0776-3 (ePub)
    978-1-4411-2321-3 (PDF)

Library of Congress Cataloging-in-Publication Data
Worley, Peter.
    The if Odyssey : a philosophical journey through Greek myth and storytelling for 8-16 year-olds / Peter Worley ; illustrated by Tamar Levi.
        p. cm.
    Includes bibliographical references and index.
    ISBN 978-1-4411-7495-6 -- ISBN 978-1-4411-0776-3 -- ISBN 978-1-4411-2321-3 1. Storytelling. 2. Homer. Odyssey. 3. Mythology, Greek--Study and teaching (Elementary) 4. Mythology, Greek--Study and teaching (Secondary) 5. Philosophy--Study and teaching (Elementary) 6. Philosophy--Study and teaching (Secondary) 7. Interdisciplinary approach in education. I. Title.
    LB1042.W67 2012
    372.67'7--dc23

                                                            2012021019

Typeset by Fakenham Prepress Solutions, Fakenham, Norfolk NR21 8NN
Printed and bound in Great Britain

For Emma, who listened and who listens, and for Katie, for whom the odyssey has only just begun. With the deepest love.

Contents

'Sing, Muse, the story of that resourceful man who was driven to wander far and wide after he had sacked the holy citadel of Troy.'
From the opening lines of the *Odyssey* by Homer

'Summon our divine bard, Demodocus; a god has given him the special gift of delighting our ears with his song, at whatever point he chooses to begin.'
King Alcinous of Phaeacia from the *Odyssey* by Homer

Foreword

The enduring appeal of Homer's *Odyssey* is easy to understand. The tale of one man's struggle to return home from the long war in Troy offers battles, betrayal, fidelity, seduction, riddles and puzzles, fearsome monsters, deceptive goddesses and beguiling nymphs. Once heard, the stories of the Wooden Horse, The Cyclops, Circe and the Pigs, Tiresias and the Underworld and Scylla and Charybdis remain deep within us, a treasure-trove for life. In the ancient world, these stories were also deployed for moral instruction: how to keep battling for what you believe in, against all the odds; how to resist the Sirens' enchantment or the tempting euphoria provided by the juice of the lotus fruit. Both their appeal and their pedagogic importance were heightened by the fact that children and adults alike would often have heard the stories told by a skilled rhapsode: tone of voice, facial expression and gesture would all have made the stories come alive. It is through this experience, of shared re-enactment and shared listening, that the *Odyssey* bestows its greatest gifts.

In *The If Odyssey*, Peter Worley gives modern schoolchildren the chance to enjoy and learn from the *Odyssey* in this way. He provides teachers with guidance that is both inspirational and refreshingly practical, and which will help them retell the stories in ways that will engage and stimulate their students' imaginations, and also provide a springboard for debate on the cultural, historical and above all philosophical issues raised: happiness and pleasure; law and lawlessness; personal identity; free will, chance and fate; the notion of the hero. The fact that the *Odyssey* is a story, containing many stories within it, makes it particularly suitable for raising questions about the relation between ethics and narrative: what is the shape of a good, well-lived life overall and what sort of person do you have to be to live this life? How important are role models and examples in general in helping us understand such questions and put possible answers into practice? Can the 'same' story be told from different points of view? Do some values and practices only make sense when seen within the context of a particular community?

The If Odyssey addresses all these issues and more, but so skilfully and entertainingly that – as I know from watching a class in action – the students will want to be active participants in the retellings and subsequent discussions. To help build the teachers' confidence (and thereby the students' confidence), every possible resource is provided: hints on effective storytelling; clear and concise summaries of the tales; keyword lists to aid memory; help with the pronunciation of names; questions for the philosophical discussions; even a guide to the Greek alphabet for those wishing to take things further.

I strongly share Peter Worley's belief that the treasures of the *Odyssey* are for all people and all time, and I also share his passionate commitment to the value of children acquiring the basics of conceptual analysis and reasoned argument. All children deserve to have their lives enriched, informed and stimulated by both Homer and philosophy, and *The If Odyssey* is the perfect introduction to both.

Professor Angie Hobbs
Professor of the Public Understanding of Philosophy
Sheffield University

Acknowledgements

First of all, thanks to Melanie Wilson and Rosie Pattinson at Continuum for their work in bringing this book to print. A huge thank you to Philosophy Foundation specialist Robert Torrington for running the sessions from notes delivered over the phone each week and for our wonderful conversations about how to best shape the narrative and run the sessions; especial thanks for his recommendations for Chapter 13: The Storyteller; and thanks to Rob's Ashmead Year 5 class about whom a British Museum guide said they had displayed the greatest knowledge of the Ancient World that he had come across in a class of their age. A special thank you also goes to Oliver Leech whose detailed notes really improved the book (and the English) and who gave me the initial idea to search the entire *Odyssey* for philosophy beyond the few stories I was then using; and to my wife Emma for her extensive help (editing and formatting), support and incredible juggling skills. Thanks to Miriam Cohen and Andrew Day and teacher Richard Toynton for their encouraging remarks about the project, and Richard also for the idea of the Briar Rose extension activity at the end of The Underworld session and for suggesting pronunciation guidance for the Greek names. Thanks to Tamar Levi and Tim Bradford for wonderful illustrations and cover art – *thanks Tamar for working so hard and efficiently*! And thanks to 11-year-old Anna Gunstone, Alfie Bragg (12) and Jessica Ebner (9) for their reviews of the sample chapter for the proposal. Thanks also to Lorraine Worley LRSM for advice on breathing, posture and projection; to Kim Smith for the idea of using the first story for a discussion of a just war; to Philip Cowell for his support of the project; to Fay Edwards for Ancient Greek advice; to Claire Field for a crucial improving observation in the Scylla and Charybdis session; and to Wendy Turgeon for her last minute advice before going to press. Perhaps the biggest thanks should go to all the children that I, and others, have run these sessions with for making sure the sessions are as good as I am able to get them.

Preface

My first use of the *Odyssey* for philosophical purposes was the story of the Sirens as a way of getting the children to discuss 'freedom' and 'second-order desire' (see Chapter 9 on page 95). At that time I wasn't telling the story but sketching it, as philosophers tend to, with what has been called a 'stick man scenario' – describing a situation with non-specific, hollow characters and retaining only the salient features for the 'thought experiment'. But there was something that didn't make sense: *why did Odysseus have himself tied to the mast when he could just as easily have put wax in his ears too?* His solution to the problem of the Sirens seemed overcomplicated and untidy. I invented my own narrative solution in an attempt to tidy it up: that the men needed to be able to tell when the danger had passed and Odysseus would give them some kind of indication from his physical demeanour. But this, too, was somewhat clumsy – why does it follow that his demeanour would indicate anything? I would only understand why things were as they were in the story when I *got to know* Odysseus through learning the other stories. He had himself tied to the mast in order to hear the music and survive and this only makes sense when you understand Odysseus' character: that he's proud, arrogant, resourceful, risk-taking – he wants his cake and he wants to eat it!

This anecdote also helps to understand the importance of narrative when trying to understand other complex situations or problems. This is the position of a branch of ethics known as 'narrative ethics' that stands in direct contrast to the 'stick man ethics' of familiar philosophical problems such as 'the trolley problem' (see Chapter 10 on page 103 and its accompanying online section). *Removing context*, some critics of 'the stick man' approach say, *makes the example significantly artificial and it therefore loses its real-world power.* So, it is for these reasons that I have combined the *Odyssey* with both philosophy and storytelling. By placing the children in the story-world of the *Odyssey* they are able to engage in far more complex and sophisticated ethical and philosophical discussions than they would otherwise be able to do.

Readers may notice that in *The If Odyssey* there are some changes to Homer's original narrative. It may be helpful to say a few words about this. In this book I have tried to achieve a balance between three things: 1) retelling the tale, 2) telling it in a way that is approachable and engaging for young people and 3) allowing philosophy to be done as easily as possible through the stories.

Given that the overall aim of this book is to do philosophy through the story of the Odyssey, where changes have been made to the original story, this is in order to meet the philosophical aims. In most cases the changes are slight – for example, in the story of Circe and The Pig Men I inserted an extra narrative part of my own in which the men have to choose to return to their human form or not. This allows into the story the classic philosophical dilemma of whether it is better to be a happy pig or an unhappy human. Probably the most significant change is the introduction of a completely new character called 'Leetho' in Chapter 13: The Storyteller (actually, Leetho is really Odysseus but with memory loss and so renamed by Nausicaa). This alteration allows for the classic discussion of personal identity and memory.

Although I have tried to include as much of the original tale as possible, there are also a small number of 'storytelling changes' I have made. For instance, the reference to 'a shroud' for Odysseus' father Laertes in the section with Penelope and the suitors has been changed, in line with many other retellings, to 'a tapestry'. This is because I thought the shroud opened up narrative questions for my audience that were distracting ('Who is Laertes?' 'Is he dead?' 'Why is she making a shroud for Odysseus' father?' etc.) As a storyteller, the reader is welcome to reinstate the original features as they see fit, and one of the wonderful things about storytelling is that this is easy enough to do. However, most of the changes I have made help to facilitate the philosophical enquiries with your class so I hope you'll forgive occasional liberties that have been made with the narrative.

I have in no way exhausted the discussion possibilities of the *Odyssey* in this book. I have chosen to highlight philosophical issues and discussions in this retelling because of the aims of this book, but you may use it to engender and follow further discussions not mentioned here.

It should also be noted that the position of this author is not to use storytelling to instil values, as they have been used for millennia, but to *critically engage* an audience. The listeners are encouraged to respond and react, to become active participants in the generation of what it is they are to get from the stories, not passive vessels for the stories to fill with received opinions and values.

As an incentive to learn to *tell* the *Odyssey*, remember that once you have told the stories a few times they will stay with you and become your own. Once you have completed the cycle you will be the proud owner of a fairly thorough version of the *Odyssey* bound only within the jacket cover of your head. Then, hopefully, you will ask, 'Why stop at the *Odyssey*?'

Peter Worley
May 2012
The Philosophy Foundation
London

Introduction

What you will find in *The If Odyssey*

There are three main sections to *The If Odyssey* and an online supplement.

Introduction

A comprehensive, explanatory introduction that gives an overview of how to use the book.

Section 1: Classroom Techniques for *The If Odyssey*

Ariadne: The Art of Facilitation – A quick guide to the facilitation skills needed to run the philosophical enquiries.

Aoidos: The Lost Art of Storytelling – An introduction to storytelling the *Odyssey* and an explanation of *Storykit*: a starter-kit for teacher-storytellers.

Logos: Teaching Strategies – An introduction to key strategies for encouraging deeper thinking in the classroom.

Section 2: The *Odyssey*

Each Chapter in this section includes:

- A short introduction to the salient philosophical/Ancient Greek themes that the story raises to help the teacher engage with the issues before introducing them to the children.
- A *Storykit* section, which has the following icon:

And also includes:

- A list of names of characters and places that should be known by the storyteller, including a pronunciation guide.
- A keyword suggestion list to help the storyteller with memorisation and prompting.
- A *hints* section sharing key storytelling skills for the budding storyteller.

- A synopsis of the story as a reminder for the storyteller.
- A fully written-out version of each story from the *Odyssey*, either to be read or as guidance to the storyteller for their own telling of the *Odyssey*.
- A Philosophical Enquiry (PhiE) based on themes from the story. This comes with a lesson plan and guidance for use in the classroom. This section is highlighted with the following icon: ⚆
- Many Chapters also contain Extension Activities for cross-curricula work and Advanced PhiE's for older children.

Section 3: After the *Odyssey*

Section 3 contains some further stories and extension activities for use during or after your telling of the *Odyssey* that includes a complete beginner's workshop for learning Ancient Greek.

Online Supplement

The online supplement on the companion website includes:

- A separate philosophy section *Through The Philosopher's Eye* (to be printed out or projected) for selected Chapters. This online supplement introduces more of the history of philosophy directly to the pupils through the characters of Katina and Zander and is aimed at the older and/or more able students. This is in a conversational style to encourage an interactive approach to thinking through some of the underlying philosophy. Where you see the Talk Time icon – ⚆ – encourage discussion, either in pairs, groups and/ or a full-class PhiE. They are suggestions only, so use your judgement about when you allow discussions to occur. Chapters that have a *Through The Philosopher's Eye* section will have the online icon at the beginning of the Chapter: ⚆
- Two back-to-back versions of the synopses (full synopses and a three-point synopsis of each Chapter for quick reference) and the full *Storykit* manual are all available in one section for easy reference.
- Printable *Keyword lists* of each story for the storyteller.
- Maps plotting Odysseus' progress around the Mediterranean to show to a class. There are also maps that include the stories The Ciconians and The Laestrygonians for older children and there are maps that omit these stories for the younger children.
- *The Words of Tiresias* – a poem for projection and/or for printing-out so that the students are engaged in trying to make sense of the story before it happens.
- The speeches of Eurylochus made during Chapter 11: The Cattle of Helios for projection. (These are required for the lesson plan.)

• Winged Word Worksheets for the Ancient Greek workshops including the Ancient Greek alphabet and pronunciation guide (see Appendices 2, 3 and 4)

Who is this book for?

The If Odyssey has been written primarily for teachers, though it will be of use to anyone working with children between the ages of 8 and 16 years who wants to introduce the children to this great set of tales. This may include teachers of history, philosophy, classics, literature and drama. The book can be used as:

• A storytelling resource and guide for telling the *Odyssey* and for learning basic Ancient Greek words and symbols.
• A vehicle for doing philosophy (PhiE method) / introduction to philosophy with children and teenagers.
• A resource for Community of Enquiry sessions ('P4C' method).
• A text-version of the *Odyssey* appropriate to be read to – or with – younger people (ages 8–16).
• It may even be read by children (or adults) as an introduction to the *Odyssey* and/or philosophy.

Meeting the curriculum needs

There are plenty of opportunities to make these stories cross-curricular. For instance, geography can be taught using the maps of Greece and of Odysseus' journey that can be found online; Ancient Greek symbols, alphabet and words can be taught (see 'Learning Ancient Greek', page xxiv); the stories can be used to teach other topics and subjects through the Extension Activities such as creative writing, research and literacy. Where they have been noticed, I have included appropriate cross-curricular oppor-tunities, such as the introduction of a mathematical average in The Cattle of Helios session.

The 'teacher-teller'

Though professional storytellers should find this a useful resource for tell-able, but also fairly comprehensive, versions of the stories of the *Odyssey*, the storytelling part of the book is aimed first and foremost at teachers. Professional storytellers make wonderful use of extraneous components to enhance their storytelling, the use of an alter ego, costumes, props, and so on. However, I think these can act as barriers to getting the teacher storytelling, so I present the craft of storytelling in a pared-down way. On occasion, I suggest ways that the teacher can make use of props or role-play, for instance, but these are offered as ways the teacher can further develop their storytelling – as optional extras rather than essential features of the storyteller's craft. Any teacher is, of course, welcome to turn up to class dressed in a toga and false beard and announce that they are Homer (and *not* Mrs Smith!) complete with a storyteller's stick and lyre. However, if you find this prospect uncongenial then I hope you will feel encouraged if I say that, though this can be done to great effect, it is not necessary. You can be an excellent teacher-storyteller with none of the frills. The *desire to tell*, having *something to tell* and having *someone to tell who wants to listen* are all you need to start incorporating stories and storytelling into your teaching. This book offers hints and tips to build from these basic starting points – and to ensure that the third condition holds. The only prop that's needed for the prospective 'teacher-teller' is him-or-herself.

How to use this book

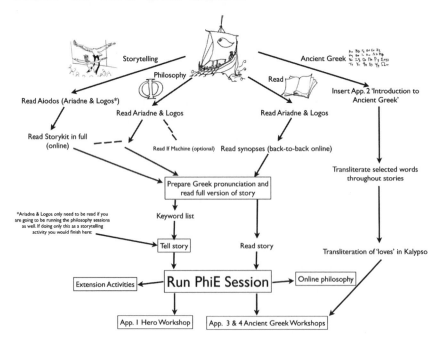

How you approach this book depends very much on what you want to achieve with it. If, for instance, you want to run the philosophy sessions then it is advisable to read *The Art of Facilitation* (page 3) carefully before progressing to the sessions themselves. For more on the art of philosophy facilitation, see my book *The If Machine: Philosophical Enquiry in the Classroom*. Much of what is contained in the chapter 'The Art of Facilitation' is a précis of the material you will find in *The If Machine*.

If you plan to use the book to build your storytelling skills, then it is advisable to read all the *Storykit* material (available all together online) before beginning. I hope that most who read *The If Odyssey* are planning to tell the stories *and* run the philosophy sessions. In which case, you should read all of Section 1 before beginning to use the Section 2 material in practice. Once you are ready to start reading or telling the stories, read the synopses to get an overview of the entire epic without having to read all the Chapters. But be warned! Each synopsis is not structured dramatically. It is just the plot, so don't use this as the model for delivery. That will come from the full versions and the accompanying *Keyword lists*. You will find the synopses in full, consecutive order on the companion website.

A shortcut to the storytelling

If you are really pushed for time, as most teachers are, and you just want to get started, then you may be able to 'get by' if you follow these steps:

1 Turn to the first story/session, then read it through carefully.
2 Use the *Keyword list* to test that you know the story and run through it in your head.
3 Put the *Keyword list* down and try again without it, looking only when necessary to jog your memory.
4 Tell the story to your class, stopping for the PhiE sections where indicated (the PhiE sections don't have to be memorised). Again, look to your Keyword list only when necessary.
5 Make reflective notes on your telling and flick to the section (see *Storykit Hint* in the contents page) that addresses your weaknesses for helpful hints. If, for example, you find your fact-recall was strong but your description and atmosphere-building was weak, then turn to 'Describing your story and building an atmosphere' on page 59 for some helpful hints and exercises on how to build an atmosphere.

So, rather than 'read then do it', this way you 'do it then read it' and although this is not the ideal way to use *The If Odyssey*, it is a suggested time-efficient method if you are really pressed for time and are feeling relatively confident.

Reading the stories

Although *The If Odyssey* has been written with storytelling in mind, you are not forbidden to *read* it to – or with – your class. In fact, I have taken some considerable care with the language so that it can serve both as a model for prospective 'tellers' and so that it can be read.

The philosophical enquiries

The philosophy sessions are integrated into the stories and you will find the explanation of how to run each philosophical enquiry (*PhiE*) in each Chapter indicated by a *PhiE* symbol:

When you see this, stop telling or reading the story and follow the guidance for the *PhiE*. Once you have finished the enquiry then continue with the story. Instead of using the session plans provided, you may want to put together your own questions for the stories to meet your own curriculum needs, or you may want to conduct a *Community of Enquiry* around the stories, allowing the children to generate their own questions for the enquiries.

The maps

Online, there are maps of Odysseus' progress. Project or print-off whichever map describes their current position and progress, but to engage the children with the maps geographically, you could set them the task of finding the corresponding modern place names of the scenes of the mythical adventure.

Chapter titles

The Chapters have been given creative titles (e.g. 'The War') for use with classes so that they don't tell the children what's about to happen or which story it is. But for ease of reference I have included, in parentheses, the more well-known story titles (e.g. 'The Wooden Horse') and I will use these titles for reference throughout the book precisely because they are informative for the teacher. *Note*: when I tell the stories I don't refer to titles at all, but they are good to use if you are *reading* them.

How to structure your telling of the *Odyssey*

The If Odyssey should cover around a term's worth of sessions, if you run a session a week. Here is a suggested term-plan (12 weeks) for the *Odyssey*:

Week 1:   The Wooden Horse
Week 2:   The Lotus Eaters
Week 3:   The Cyclops
Week 4:   Aeolus
Week 5:   Circe
Week 6:   The Underworld
Week 7:   The Sirens
Week 8:   Scylla and Charybdis
Week 9:   Calypso
Week 10: The Phaeacians
Week 11: The Return Home
Week 12: Ancient Greek Workshop/The Hero

I have told the *Odyssey* without two of the stories, The Ciconians and The Laestrygonians, for some time; they contain events and themes you may not feel as comfortable with (the slaughter of a town's people and cannibalism), especially with younger children. I added them into the book as they seemed to me to raise very philosophical issues that work very well with secondary school students and possibly final-year primary students. See the notes about them in their respective Chapters for more on the appropriateness of these sessions. Insert them – if you decide to – only if you have time or want to look at the issues therein specifically. You are welcome to run the entire series of stories and workshops, but bear in mind that this is likely to be more than a term's worth of work, though it can be done within a term if you run more than one session per week. The Ancient Greek Workshop (see Appendix 3) can be inserted wherever you like, or replaced with The Hero (see Appendix 1) session if you are not doing the Ancient Greek component, though this should be done only at the end. If you only have half a term to do the *Odyssey* then I suggest the following half-term plans (choose either A or B), although you can make your own plan to fit your own aims:

	A		B
	Week 1: The Wooden Horse		Week 1: The Wooden Horse
	Week 2: The Lotus Eaters		Week 2: The Cyclops
	Week 3: Aeolus		Week 3: Circe/The Underworld
	Week 4: Circe/The Underworld		Week 4: The Sirens
	Week 5: The Sirens		Week 5: Scylla and Charibdis
	Week 6: The Return Home		Week 6: Kalypso (and a quick Return)

A good deal of 'filling in' and précising will need to be done when shortening in this way, but minimise any summary to what is absolutely necessary for the narrative to make sense. I have run half of the stories in one year and the other half the following year. It's amazing what the children can remember!

Learning Ancient Greek

This book also includes an introduction to Ancient Greek for children. It has been done with children in primary school from Year 3 (age 7) to Year 6 (age 11).

The Ancient Greek workshop can be found on Appendix 3 and is based around another Greek story, *Oidipus and The Riddle of the Sphinx* (I have stuck to the phonetic pronunciation and spelling of **oi**-di-pus, as opposed to the usual **ee**-di-pus/Oedipus, to help with transliteration). Here, as with the Kalypso session, translation becomes necessary for the story to progress – an important way for stories to be used for learning, it should be noted.

A note on pronouncing Ancient Greek: in the pronunciation guide I have written in **bold** the syllable that is to be accented. However, it is worth noting that this is how I accent the word. Exactly how Ancient Greeks accented their words is to some extent mysterious given that Ancient Greek is no longer a spoken language. The pronunciations given are for guidance only and if you feel strongly that a word should be pronounced differently then pronounce it as you see fit, as long as you are consistent in your practice.

A quick word about Ancient Greek sexuality

You may feel uncomfortable with the explicit sexuality, violence and general gruesomeness in Greek mythology. Homer's *Odyssey* is no exception, being sexual, violent and gruesome in equal measure – though, unlike the *Iliad*, containing only heterosexual encounters. I have removed the explicitness but retained an echo of the sexuality (for instance the offer by Kalypso to satisfy all Odysseus' wants). I have, on occasion retained some gruesome scenes to increase their emotional impact (notably the consumption of crew-members by the sea monster Scylla). Storytelling allows the teller to make decisions about what to retain and what to excise according to the age of the class. If setting 'research questions' then the children are very likely to uncover aspects of Ancient Greek sexuality, particularly their acceptance and celebration of homosexuality. I shall not tell you what to say on this – just that it is worth being prepared for. One way to deal with this, especially with older children, may be to explain this feature of Ancient Greek culture before they surprise you with it. The *Odyssey* may also provide an excellent opportunity to broach these tricky subjects in an appropriate and mature way.

Section 1
Classroom Techniques
for *The If Odyssey*

Ariadne: The Art of Facilitation

In the book *The If Machine* I made metaphorical use of another Greek myth, that of Ariadne, Theseus and the labyrinth, to make two points about facilitation: the twin ideas of *absence* and *navigation*. You may recall that Ariadne provided Theseus with the tools for navigating his way out of the maze but was crucially not there when he did so. Good facilitation is about the extent to which you are *not present* as much as it is about your *effective presence* and that the artistry is in getting that balance right: being 'present but hidden'. This section will provide a summary of good facilitation practices that can be found in more detail in *The If Machine*, but if you do not have access to the other book then this should give you what you need to begin the art of facilitation.

Quick guide on how to run a PhiE session using *The If Odyssey*

1 *The Talking Circle*: Sit your class in a circle or horseshoe shape. Eye contact is very important if you want successful discussion-based sessions.
2 *Tell your story*. See the *Storykit* section for suggestions of how to do this effectively.
3 *The PhiE Section*: Stop the story at the appropriate time as indicated in the chapters to run the PhiE part of the session. You do not need to memorise this part.
4 *Task Question*: Do any necessary set-up, then ask the Task Question (abbreviated to 'TQ' from here on), writing it up clearly on the board.
5 *Talk Time*: Allow two minutes or so where the children speak to each other in pairs or small groups. Take this opportunity to find out what individuals think.
6 *Gain their attention*: After a couple of minutes of Talk Time use a visual signal explained at the outset to get the class's attention.
7 *Begin The Enquiry*: Remind them of the TQ and begin the enquiry (see speaker management below).
8 *Facilitate the Enquiry*: Allow as many of the children as possible to speak – though it should not be mandatory – and use the basic strategy of 'anchoring and opening up' or 'if-ing, anchoring and opening up' (see page 18) to facilitate the discussion. But remember *not to say what you think*! Your job is to facilitate a dialogic discussion between the children – one that is structured, disciplined and rigorous, and that is built naturally and step-by-step from comments and responses made by the children.
9 *New Task Questions*: If a new TQ emerges from the discussion, or you want to move to a further TQ from the book, then set the new TQ and repeat the process from step 4.
10 *Finish the story*: If necessary, leave enough time to continue with what's left of the story before ending the session.

Getting to the heart of the matter from 'in the story' to 'out of the story'

A good starting place for a PhiE is a concrete question, one that is clearly grounded 'in the story'. The question 'Should Odysseus drink the juice or not?' in The Lotus Eaters session (page 39) is a question of this sort. However, a good philosophical enquiry (and the mark of a good philosophy facilitator) is one that moves from the concrete to the abstract, in other words, from 'in the story' to 'out of the story'. Questions such as 'Is happiness the most important thing?' are abstracted 'out of the story' and are much more general questions about the nature of the value of happiness. These kinds of question get to the heart of the matter and are less likely to run into irrelevance. For example, I have heard discussions around the following question: 'If there was a pill that made you always happy would you – or should you – eat it?' where the children's concern moved from 'the importance of happiness' to 'whether you should eat things when you don't know where they have been?' The Nested Questions in each Chapter lists further questions that could provide opportunities to move the discussion 'out of the story' and closer to the heart of the matter, philosophically speaking. However, in order to make the discussions accessible, many of the starting Task Questions begin 'in the story'.

Speaker management

I like to pass a ball to speakers so that there is a clear visual indication of whose go it is. However, there are many ways that speakers can be managed. The standard method is to ask for 'hands up those who want to speak'. But beware! This method alone – as with any single method of speaker management – will result in only a certain group of children contributing. Change your speaker management method periodically to enable different speakers to access the discussion – the aim (though not the *requirement*) being to have everyone contribute during a session. For instance, why don't you occasionally ask for hands down and then 'pass the ball randomly', making sure that they know they can pass the ball back if they really don't want to say something (*random selection method*)? Or, why don't you ask for hands up from 'only those who have something to say in response to the last speaker' (*response-detector method*)? There are many other kinds of speaker management methods, so research, find out more and try things out (see *The If Machine* 'Speaker Management' for much more on this). The key is: keep changing your speaker management method, but not too often.

Key facilitation questions to ask yourself to help monitor your own progress

- 'Would an observer know what I think about the issue under discussion?' (They *shouldn't* be able to tell.)
- 'Have the children said back to me what *I think* rather than what *they think*?' (Again, they *shouldn't* know what you think.)

- 'What *questions* can I ask to move things on?'
- 'Is there any information I need to *teach* for the discussion to be able to develop?' (Remember to minimise teaching during *PhiE* discussions.)
- 'Are there any *strategies* I can use to help develop this discussion?' (For example, *Carve it up* on page 16 or *Break the Circle* on page 15, etc. See *The If Machine* for many more.)
- 'How can I get the children to challenge – *for themselves* – a point raised in the discussion?' (Try not to do this yourself.)
- 'Do they need some *Talk Time*?'
- 'Am I talking too much? Are they talking enough?'
- 'Are the children putting their hands up? If not, why not?'
- 'Is the Task Question clear?' (Clearly articulated and written up.)
- 'Do I need to introduce a new Task Question?' (Either from the Nested Questions list or as an emerging question from the discussion.)

Aoidos: The Lost Art of Storytelling

It was not an arbitrary decision to combine the *Odyssey* with storytelling. First of all, the *Odyssey* was told as part of an oral tradition in Ancient Greece for many hundreds of years before it was eventually written down. The written version that we know was therefore the product of a storytelling tradition. Second, Homer is also something of a mythological character having been 'storied' to a greater or lesser extent himself, there being reason to believe that Homer in fact lived hundreds of years before either the *Iliad* or the *Odyssey* were written down.

The links to storytelling are not just historical but can be found threaded throughout the story itself. We find that the *Odyssey* begins with the words 'Tell me' – an appeal from the storyteller to the Muse to give the storyteller the story. The character of Demodocus, himself a blind storyteller, mirrors the portrait we have of Homer, also thought to be blind. During the scene of feasting in the court of Alcinous, Demodocus has to cease his storytelling in order to hand over to 'Odysseus the storyteller'. This means that we find, within the *Odyssey*, that wonderfully reflexive feature of 'a story within a story' where *the teller* is also the *told of*. At one point we, the readers, are *told the story* of Odysseus (by the narrator who is in turn being told the story by the Muse) *telling the story* of Eurylochus *telling the story* of the men having been changed into pigs by Circe.

I have included at least one of the *Storykit Hints* in each Chapter and have selected the skill most relevant to that Chapter. You can, however, access all the *Storykit* material consecutively online. Below you will find some more general points about storytelling that are not skills and so have not been included in the *Storykit Hint* sections.

Refrains

A characteristic feature of a story and the art of the storyteller is the use of *refrains* or *choruses* (for example, 'Fee-fie-fo-fum' in the English tale *Jack and The Beanstalk*) and ready-made sentences, the most well-known to modern audiences being 'Once upon a time ...'. Refrains and choruses are repeated phrases that give a story a song-like quality and help to sew the story together. Ready-made sentences are a signal to the audience that they should expect a certain kind of thing. Though the *Odyssey* doesn't contain any choruses, such as the 'Fee-fie-fo-fum' example, it does have certain ready-made sentences that are repeated throughout the narrative. I have taken most of these out of my version but include some of them here for any teller who may want to reinsert them.

- *'When Dawn came, fresh and rosy-fingered ...'* – To be said whenever you want to say 'morning came'. *Note*: For the Ancient Greeks, many features of the natural world, such as dawn, are personified in a god, indicated here with a capital letter for 'Dawn'.
- *'the wine-dark sea ...'* – The Greeks did not have the rich range of colour-words that we have, and there is reason to believe that they conceived of or possibly even perceived colour differently to us.
- *'resourceful Odysseus'* – This is a useful phrase to use at least on occasion, perhaps when others refer to Odysseus. It is useful especially if you want to explain the wonderful play-on-words in Ancient Greek to do with 'nobody' and 'resourceful' found in the Cyclops story. (See note about *me tis* on page 54.)
- *'with heavy hearts we grieved for the loss of our friends but rejoiced at our own survival'* – Used whenever the crew undergoes a loss of life.
- *'the men struck the surf with wood'* – This seems to indicate that they rowed with determination.

- *'then he said with words that flew'* or *'said with winged words'* – By some thought to mean nothing more than 'he/she said', but by others thought to mean 'said with urgency' or 'reflecting spontaneity, surprise, insight or feeling'. It could mean 'said with a strong desire to communicate', in which case all of the storyteller's words are 'winged', or should be! (See title for the story of *Oidipus and The Riddle of The Sphinx* in Appendix 4 on page 170)

Tenses and persons

I have found that telling stories can work very well in the present tense as it can bring the story to the audience immediately without the distance of the past between them. Stories written and read in the present tense, however, can seem awkward and unnatural to many readers, especially young readers. But because these stories have been written to demonstrate *telling* rather than *reading* I have written some of them in the past tense – because I have told them in that tense. I have also included some stories in the present tense, and there is a specific reason why I have done this. It is because I want to invite the children into the story itself by asking them to imagine that they are among the crew-members of the ship. This is another way that you can use storytelling effectively to bring a story to life. It also means that the stories in which I have done this are written in the second person. This is an unusual voice for a written story but a very effective one for a told story.

However, you can tell the stories in whichever voice you prefer – another virtue of the storyteller's art. You could tell the whole thing in the third person if you wish. It is worth noting that Homer's original also plays with the 'voices'. It begins in the third person – in the voice of the narrator, but later moves through the more familiar stories (i.e. from Odysseus' leaving Troy all the way to his landing on the Phaeacian's shore) in the first person as Odysseus himself tells the stories to King Alcinous, only to resume the third person perspective for the rest of the narrative. The use of the second person also has a precedent in Homer's original when, in the chapter that introduces Eumaeus, Homer strangely begins to address Eumaeus in the second person as if he is suddenly telling the story to him. I think one possible reason why he does this is to identify the audience with the character of Eumaeus, not least because Homer clearly likes him; possibly also because the audience has the same narrative investments that he does: if you read the original you will notice how he repeatedly wishes for Odysseus' return (the audience's wish also) and for injustice to be dealt with (the audience also wish to see the suitors' comeuppance). I think this helps to emphasise the dramatic irony here, as the audience share his concerns and hopes but have more knowledge than he does. In a similar manner, *The If Odyssey* makes use of the second person perspective to help draw the audience *into* the stories by inviting them to become the crew, but this perspective cannot be maintained because the crew are all killed before the conclusion of the narrative is reached. Nevertheless, I think that switching perspectives and voices is not only in keeping with the original but also keeps the telling varied both for 'the teller' and 'the told to'.

How long should a story from *The If Odyssey* take to tell?

I give an hour to the sessions and I hope to have 30 to 40 minutes devoted to the PhiE; the rest is allotted to the storytelling. These stories take anywhere between 10 minutes (The Wooden Horse) and 30 minutes (The Cyclops) to tell, though with many of the stories there is another five minutes of telling after you've run the PhiE section. If you are only taking two minutes to tell a story like The Sirens then you are not giving enough time to the story. You could try to expand a little on detail and atmosphere (see Storykit Hint on page 59) or maybe you could try to pause a little more between sentences and paragraphs, or generally slow down. If, on the other hand, you are taking up most of the session with telling and, for instance, taking over half an hour to tell a story like The Lotus Eaters then the chances are you are expanding far too much on detail and description. The best indicator that you are taking too long is when you begin to see signs that the children are losing interest. Of course, there will often be someone who loses interest, even if only for a short time, but if there is a conspicuously large number of children losing interest and it is happening regularly then this should tell you something. *Remember*: stories have been shown time and again to be a very effective way of engaging children of all backgrounds and ages, so if your stories are failing to engage, then you might want to think again about *how you are doing it* rather than conclude that 'storytelling doesn't work for my class'! If so, turn to the *Storykit* sections of this book (see the Contents page and *Storykit* online) for hints that will help to improve your telling. You always have the backup of being able to read it if absolutely necessary.

Keyword lists

It is advisable, when learning a story for telling, that you read through the story carefully, making notes of key words that will help you to recall the events sequentially in the story (online you will find a Keyword list sheet for you to do this). Suggested Keyword lists have been provided for you before each story as part of the *Storykit* section. However, it is advisable to do your own when you can, as the act of drawing up your list will help to process the story more thoroughly.

Exercise: Keyword facts

Here is an exercise you may find helpful to do before attempting to tell a story, especially if you are inexperienced. Look at the Keyword list and ask yourself all the following questions about the characters and events that are listed. If you know 'the facts' then you are factually prepared for storytelling, but if you simply don't know the answer to 'Who is Menelaos?' or 'Why are all the Greeks sending ships to Troy when it was only Menelaos (of Sparta) that was offended by Paris' actions?' then you need to find that out, and to do that all you have to do is read the full version of the story carefully (or, if you are keen for more detailed information then consult a good classical dictionary – or Homer's original). Simply explain out loud to yourself who's who and what's what. Don't worry about descriptions at this stage, just the facts. Look at the Keyword list of one of the stories and answer these questions to each keyword/phrase:

- Who? (Characters)
- Why? (Motivation)
- Where? (Setting)
- So what? (Consequences)

This key-question list acts as a good overall formula for 'questions to ask yourself' about each of your keywords.

Key storytelling questions to ask yourself to help monitor your own progress:

- 'Are they engaged?' (Look for signs: where are they looking? Are they fidgeting? Are they yawning?, etc.)
- 'How long am I taking over each story?' (Time this!)
- 'Do I have my back to any audience members? Am I looking at people?'
- 'Is the classroom set up in the best way?'
- 'How many interruptions have there been? How can I minimise interruptions?'
- 'Am I um-ing and ah-ing?'
- 'Am I enjoying myself?'
- 'Do I look forward to storytelling?' (Or am I dreading it?!)
- 'Are there any hints in the *Storykit* that I can use to improve my storytelling?'

If you are feeling brave, you could ask your class what they think of your storytelling. It is one of the best ways to test your skills because, after all, they are your target audience. But be prepared for some brutal honesty!

Logos: Teaching Strategies for Developing Reasoning

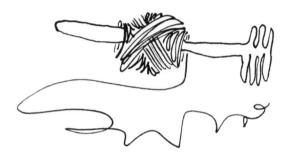

Among other things, the Ancient Greek word *logos* means 'account' or 'reason'. Earlier I said that Ariadne provided the *tools* to aid Theseus' escape from the labyrinth: a clew and thread in fact – a 'clew' being a special wooden device made by Daedelus for Theseus requested by Ariadne, that enables a thread to be run from it. The 'tools' are the strategies used to enable good discussion and good thinking/reasoning (the *logos* or 'account'). See 'Ariadne: The Art of Facilitation' on page 3 for an explanation of the techniques for running enquiries. In this section you will find a list of the *teaching thinking strategies* mentioned in this book. For a more comprehensive list then please consult *The If Machine* 'Teaching Strategies', though you will find one or two strategies in this book that are not in the earlier book. Abbreviations to be used throughout the book are shown in parentheses.

Task Questions (TQs)

These are the questions that should be asked explicitly in order to follow the session plans. They are carefully selected to bring the class to the intended area of philosophical focus, whether it be 'the value of happiness' (The Lotus Eaters) or 'the nature of love' (Kalypso). It is important therefore to make sure that these questions, if used, are asked *exactly as written*. Any small change to the question can change the nature of the discussion significantly.

Nested Questions

In contrast to the Task Questions, Nested Questions are the implicit questions that lie behind a discussion. For example, if the TQ is 'Is it fair to punish everyone for what one person did?' then the Nested Questions might be 'What is fair?' and 'What is punishment?', and so on. Having a list of Nested Questions is important for you to be prepared for the enquiry. Having an idea of the 'conceptual landscape' of the discussion means that you are less likely to 'blank' and not know 'where things are going' or where they can go. During the discussion, children are likely to stumble upon some of the Nested Questions, in which case, feel at liberty to turn a nested question into a Task Question. Also, make notes of questions that are neither Task nor Nested Questions but nevertheless emerge from the discussion, from ideas the children introduce. Because of the student-centred approach of a *PhiE*, these questions should often be made explicit (i.e. turned into Task Questions). These 'emergent questions' should be added to your list of Nested Questions in preparation for later sessions. In this way the list of Nested Questions for each session should, over time, grow.

Talk Time

Whenever a Task Question – or Emergent/Nested Question – is put to the class, always allow some Talk Time: 'two minutes' for the children to talk to each other on the question either in pairs or small groups. The number of people talking in each group is not so important. The only rule is that *everyone should be talking to at least one other person*. Note that this is a good time to find out what the quiet children think, since not everyone is initially comfortable sharing ideas with the whole class. Make especial use of the *Imaginary disagreer* strategy (see below) with pairs or groups in Talk Time.

Imaginary disagreer

This is a teaching thinking strategy that can be used in all sorts of different ways that asks a child, or children, to imagine that there is someone who disagrees with them. This helps to encourage them actively to seek alternative points of view. If you have two children, for example, during Talk Time, who both agree with each other and have therefore ceased to think about the issue, simply ask them to imagine that *if* there was someone in the room who disagreed with them, then what do they think he or she would say. The next step is to ask them what *reasons* they think their 'imaginary disagreer' would give. This can be used with pairs, groups and also with the whole class: see *Split debates* below. Sometimes the children will change their own minds because of what their 'disagreer' said!

Break the circle

A Socratic Question, so called because of the frequency with which the philosopher Socrates used them, is of the form 'What is F?' where 'F' stands for whatever concept is under investigation. Examples of Socratic Questions are 'What is justice?' or 'What is courage?' In the list of nested questions included in every PhiE lesson-plan you will find a Socratic Question on each of the themes found in the sessions, for example, 'What is happiness?' in The Lotus Eaters and Circe, and 'What is love?' in Kalypso.

Break the circle is based on the Socratic Question and can be employed to circumvent a classic obstacle to using Socratic Questions in enquiries. The obstacle is that children have a habit of engaging in circular thinking. For example, if you ask children what *growth* is, they will often reply with, 'It's when something grows.' Here is a game to help break the circular thinking habit. Choose a word from the list below and ask the children to tell you what the word means, but then say that there is a catch: 'You mustn't use the word in your answer.' Write up, on the top left-hand side of the board: 'It is ...' to help them stick to this stipulation, then give them some Talk Time in pairs. After a minute or two, ask them to share their answers with the class, concept-mapping (see below) as you go.

- Think
- Love
- Mind
- Grow
- Try
- Do
- Number

Once the children have been introduced to the game, you can use the technique at any time when a child provides a definition or explains a word or term or if you want to explore a concept more deeply.

Carve it up: drawing distinctions

One of the most important tools in any philosopher's toolbox is the ability to identify and then draw distinctions. For example, the ability to notice when a concept such as *freedom* needs to be carved up into further more subtle concepts such as *mental freedom* and *physical freedom*, as in the example in Chapter 9: The Sirens on page 95. Drawing distinctions is one very useful way to clarify one's thinking on an issue. If, for instance, you are having a discussion with someone about freedom but disagree about something, it may turn out that the disagreement hinges on different meanings of 'free' that each of you have. One of you may have meant 'mental freedom', for instance, but the other 'physical freedom'. Once distinctions have been drawn you can both move on in the discussion, aware of the conceptual difference you have.

To encourage the children to draw distinctions in the classroom, all you have to do is notice when they may each be using a different meaning of a single word, such as 'free' or 'good' or 'love'. Clues that this is happening are often indicated in the following kinds of comments: '*In a way* he is free and *in a way* he's not ...', or 'It's half and half ...', or 'Well, yes *and* no ...'. If they do not explicitly identify the distinctions themselves, then you can ask the following question: 'Do you think there are different meanings of the word '_____' in this discussion?' If they say 'Yes' then ask them: 'What do you think they are?' This is a very good habit for them to get into and once you have introduced this strategy to them they will probably start to draw distinctions themselves, unprompted.

Extension Activity: Carve it up

Take any word, such as the ones on the following list:

- Love
- Good
- Free
- Luck

The task is simply to identify as many different kinds of the chosen word as possible using a concept map. This can be done as a full class activity on any word under consideration or it can be done in groups or teams and given a competitive motivation. This extension activity is called 'carve it up' because you are asking the children to carve up the single word, such as 'good', into many different concepts such as '*moral* goodness' or 'being good *at* something' or 'being good *for* a purpose'. This is known as *drawing distinctions* (see above) and is an example of what philosophers call *conceptual analysis*.

Concept map

The simplest example of this is where you write a single word, for the concept under investigation, in the centre of the board, such as 'Fair', 'Beauty' or 'Love'. In order to unpack the concept and/or to explore the class's understanding of the concept, you should write up all their attempts to say what they think the said concept is or means. An example of a concept map is as follows.

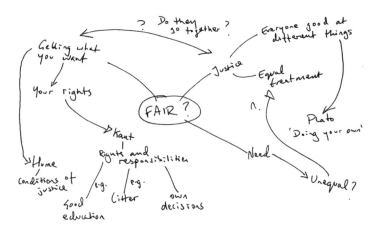

Key things to bear in mind are that you should use these only as an *aid* to PhiE discussions, so make sure that they don't become a barrier: don't worry too much about presentation and punctuation, for example. You can also write up full statements or questions in the centre of the board and then focus on the contained, relevant concepts; for example, 'Is the voluntary prisoner free?' where the relevant concepts would be 'voluntary', 'prisoner' and 'free'. (See *Break the Circle* above.)

Note: Concept maps are different to *dictionary definitions*. To help make this point, I'd like to recall an outcome of a number of philosophy sessions I've been witness to. During discussions on concepts like 'time' or 'existence' it is quite common for someone, at some point, to suggest that the issue can be resolved by looking it up in the dictionary. I always invite the class to do this and, when it has been done, I ask them if the dictionary definition answers their question. As one 11-year-old girl said in reference to the concept of 'existence' where the definition read '*to do with being*', she exclaimed 'But there's more to it than that!' And so the concept-building and discussion continued.

If it, Anchor it, Open it up!

Like a Swiss army knife, this is *three-strategies-in-one* and, like a Swiss army knife, it is a strategy to keep on you at all times.

If-ing

'If-ing' is a form of questioning that makes use of the conditional sentence structure ('if ... then ...') in order to engender hypothetical thinking. Here is an example statement and question:

'It's okay to eat meat so why don't we eat our pets?'

Here is the same statement and question once it has been *if-ed*:

'*If* it is okay to eat meat, *then* why don't we eat our pets?'

It is worth taking the time to think about what benefits there might be to *if-ing* ideas, statements and questions. *If-ing* helps to:

- Avoid factual obstacles to a discussion.
- Keep the discussion conceptual.
- Test ideas against the Task Question.
- Test different hypotheses.
- Consider alternative points-of-view.

Anchoring

This is a deceptively simple technique where the facilitator brings the student back to the case in point by re-asking the Task Question with a neutral tone. For example:

A)   (Task Question: 'Is the man free?')
Child: 'x, y, and z ...'
Facilitator (anchoring): 'So, is he free?'
Anchoring helps to:

- Keep the discussion focused.
- Keep contributions relevant.
- Reveal hidden relevance.

- Link ideas to the Task Question.
- Avoid dismissive comments from the teacher.
- Avoid premature judgement on the part of the teacher.
- Avoid unnecessary confrontation.
- Prompt children to contribute.
- Formulate and express formal arguments.

Opening up

This is how one keeps the virtue of their questioning 'open' even if 'closed questions' are being used:

B)   (Task question: 'Is the man free?')
     Child: 'x, y, and z ...'
     Facilitator (anchoring): 'So, is he free?'
     Child: 'No.'
     Facilitator (opening up): 'Why?' (or 'Could you say more about that?'
     or 'What reason do you have for that?', etc.)
     Child: 'Because p, q and r ...'

These strategies complement each other so that they form the basis of your question-asking in the classroom. So, try 'anchoring and opening up' as with B above, or 'if-ing, anchoring and opening up' to test ideas against the task question:

C)   (Task question: 'Is the man free?')
     Child: 'x, y, and z ...'
     Facilitator (if-ing): 'So if x, y and z ... then is the man free?'
     (anchoring)
     Child: 'No.'
     Facilitator (opening up): 'Why?' (or words to that effect)
     Child: 'Because p, q and r ...'

Opening-up helps to:

- Keep discussions moving.
- Elicit more information from the speaker.
- Make use of closed-questioning techniques such as *if-ing* and *anchoring* without closing down the discussion.
- Encourage justifications from the children.
- Encourage the formulation and expression of supporting reasons (formal arguments).

Debates

See below *Split Debate* and *Walk Across Debate*. Also see *Formal Debate* on page 64 in Aeolus.

Split debate

In the example of the discussion in The Lotus Eaters (Chapter 2), if you find your class unanimous on the issue threatening to jeopardise your PhiE, then try the following:

1 Split the class in two.
2 Tell one half that they are to adopt the position of Perimedes: that *he should not drink the juice*.
3 The other half role-plays the soldier offering Odysseus the juice: they will argue that *he should drink the juice*.
4 The two class halves then spend a minute or two putting together some reasons in support of their position.
5 Then they have a dialogue across the room with each other, taking it in turns to have one speaker from each side make a contribution.
6 Halfway through, you could get them to swap positions and spend some time arguing the other side of the case.
7 At the end of the debate, each member of the group should make their own decision having heard all the reasons from both sides of the argument. They could each share their decision and their deciding reason at the end.

The walk across debate

Sometimes you may feel that the children need to get up out of their seats. If so, then try the following debate method, though it works best when you know that there are enough people to occupy both (or all three!) sides of the debate. Use this strategy wherever you feel it would be useful, for instance, when they have to decide whether to follow Circe's advice that Odysseus should not tell the crew of Scylla. Discussions that have a binary nature (e.g. X or Y, X or *not*-X) lend themselves well to debates.

1 Mark a line, using a metre ruler or something similar, about a quarter of the way across the room; do the same at the other end of the room.
2 Invite those that think X to stand at one end of the room behind the marker and those that think Y (or *not*-X) to stand at the other end of the room behind the other marker. Once in place, they should sit down on the floor.

3 There should be a place in the middle of the room, between the two ends, where those that are undecided, or who think something other than X or Y, should be able to take their places.

4 Allow children from different parts of the room to speak, taking turns as in the *Split Debate* method. Speakers should stand up.

5 Once a couple of people have spoken, allow a few seconds for children to change places if they want to. It is often a good idea to ask children who have changed places to say *why they changed places*. Reasons that motivate a change in position are often good or interesting reasons and are likely to contribute to a good dialogue. It also discourages children to move just to be with their friends if they think they will be asked to justify their move!

Section 2
The *Odyssey*

The War (The Wooden Horse) 1

Philosophy

Inspired by a lesson plan for Remembrance Day, this and the next session explore the ethics of war. Wars have happened throughout history and will probably happen for a long time to come, but since the Middle Ages, philosophers and theologians have been concerned about the justifiability of war, sometimes known as *just war theory*. This is often better understood broken down into two questions:

A) *Is it right or justifiable to go to war in the first place?* (What, in the Middle Ages was called *jus ad bellum*, in Latin.)

B) *What is it right or justifiable to do during a war once you're engaged in one?* (In Latin: *jus in bello*.)

This session (The Wooden Horse) deals with the first of these questions and the next session (The Ciconians) deals with the second.

   With younger students (ages 8 or 9), you may prefer to simply ask TQ 1 below, and possibly allow the discussion to stay only 'within the story' (see page 4 for an explanation of this). However, with children of age 10 to 16 there will be room to allow the discussion to become deeper. Follow the further suggestions listed in this Chapter with your class if you feel they are of the appropriate level.

Storykit
Names to learn in this story

- **Menelaos** (pronounced: men-a-**lay**-os): King of Sparta, brother of Agamemnon and husband of the abducted Helen.
- **Helen** (pronounced as in English): Wife of Menelaos and taken by Paris to Troy.

- **Paris** (as English): Son of Priam, brother of Hektor and abductor of Helen.
- **Odysseus** (O-**di**-see-us): Hero of the *Odyssey*, son of Laertes and Anticleia (father and mother respectively), husband of Penelope and father of Telemachus.
- **Priam** (**Pry**-um): King of Troy and father of Paris.

Keyword list

- Menelaos marries Helen ('most beautiful woman in the world!').
- Odysseus offers advice to suitors.
- Paris visits Menelaos.
- Paris takes Helen to Troy.
- Greeks attack Troy ('the face that launched a thousand ships'!).
- Ten years later ...
- Odysseus' idea.
- Greeks are gone!
- The horse approaches.
- What to do?
- King Priam and the priests.
- Take it in.
- Celebration.
- Let them in and defeat! ('Beware Greeks bearing gifts!')

Storykit Hint: Keyword lists

When putting together your own keyword list, look for a single word in each section of the story that best sums up, for you, the salient feature of that section. Try to keep the key words to no more than a word or two, though sometimes it will be necessary to write a short phrase next to the key words or in place of them. Try to reduce clutter on your cue-sheet. You may prefer to replace words with pictures depending on your own learning style. To help with memorisation, you may also want to create your own synopses-in-threes (see online).

Synopsis for The War (The Trojan Horse)

The scene is set and the background told. A war breaks out between the Greeks and the Trojans over Helen's abduction from Menelaos, the king of Sparta. The war goes on for ten years before Odysseus devises a plan to infiltrate the city of Troy. A wooden horse is left outside the city that hides Odysseus and some other Greek soldiers. After King Priam discusses what to do with his priests, the horse is taken into the city as it is thought to be a gift to the gods, and the Trojans believe that they would invite the wrath of the gods if they do not take it in. Once inside, Odysseus and his men let in the Greek army through the gates. The Trojans are defeated and the war ends.

Story

Figure 1: The most beautiful woman in the world.

This story begins in Greece when a king of one of the city-states of Greece, King Menelaos, married a woman said to be 'the most beautiful woman in the world'. Her name was Helen. But there was another man in the city of Troy, across the sea from Greece, who wanted Helen as his wife. His name was Paris. So he sailed to Greece and visited King Menelaos who invited Paris into his kingdom as a guest. But one night, Paris left with Helen and returned to Troy. No one knows if Helen was taken against her will or whether she left willingly, having fallen in love with Paris. But when Menelaos discovered that his wife was gone he was furious.

The other kings of Greek city-states had also been suitors of Helen, but when Menelaos had won her hand, it was a man named Odysseus that had persuaded them to swear an oath of allegiance for the sake of peace, promising to help out if anything should happen to her. Menelaos made use of the oath that the other kings had sworn and summoned all the kings of the city-states of Greece and demanded that they provide him with an army mighty enough to defeat Troy. A thousand Greek ships set sail for Troy and it is for this reason that Helen's beautiful face has since been known as 'the face that launched a thousand ships'. Many men set off to fight in the war and one of them was Odysseus. He was the king of Ithaca and he supplied the Greeks with many ships and men.

Figure 2: But when Menelaos discovered that his wife was gone he was furious.

Imagine you are a Greek soldier about to leave your wife and children to go and fight a war across the sea. How long might you expect to be gone? A few months? A year maybe? Two years? The Greeks expected the Trojan defeat to be swift. Once they had crossed the sea they arrived at the city of Troy and lay siege to it.

 # The ethics of war 1 (*jus ad bellum*)

TQ 1: Were the Greeks right to go to war against the Trojans?

Nested Questions

- When is it right to go to war?
- Is it ever right to go to war?
- What is a war?
- If the Greeks win, would that mean that they were right to go to war?
- If the Greeks lose, would that mean that they were wrong to go to war?
- With regard to the previous two questions, does the outcome have anything to do with whether it was right or wrong to go to war?

If you think it will help and the class is of appropriate age then, to help focus the discussion, here are some of the conditions that have been offered over the years by way of justification for war:

- War may only be undertaken by a legitimate authority. (Question: What makes a legitimate authority?)
- War may only be undertaken in a just cause. (Question: What would be a just cause?)
- War may only be undertaken as a last resort. (Question: If war is a last resort, what should be attempted first?)
- War may only be undertaken with a formal declaration of war.
- War may only be undertaken when there is a reasonable hope of success. (Question: How might you work out what a reasonable hope of success is? Does it matter if you fail?)
- War may only be undertaken as a defensive response to aggression.
- Perhaps, more controversially, it may be undertaken as a pre-emptive measure in order to avoid imminent aggression.

Are there any other conditions that could be offered as justifications for war that haven't been listed so far?

The analogy between individuals and communities

Many are likely to appeal to an analogy with how individuals should or do respond to similar situations. To explore this, explain the following situation to the class:

Imagine that someone comes along and acts aggressively towards you, your friends or your family.

> TQ 2a: Do you think that you would be right to respond aggressively to protect yourself, your friends or your family?

Now imagine that another country acts aggressively towards your country.

> TQ 2b: Do you think that you would be right to respond aggressively to protect your country?

Nested Questions

- Are the two situations the same?
- Are there any differences? If so, what would they be?
- Is an individual responsible for their own act of aggression? (For example, do they give up any rights by acting aggressively?)
- Are the people of a country responsible for the aggressive acts of their leaders?

Story continued ...

The Trojans turned out to be much tougher than the Greeks had imagined and ten years later the Greeks were still fighting the war against the Trojans. The Greeks were about to give up and go home, defeated and without Helen, when one of the Greek captains had an idea that was as extraordinary as it was brilliant. Which Greek do you think it was who had the idea? It was Odysseus.

Every morning since the beginning of the war the Trojans had looked out over the city walls to see the Greek army encamped for as far as they could see. And, in the distance, they could see a thousand Greek ships moored along the coast. And beyond that they could see the sea stretching out to the horizon. But one morning they were met with a very different picture. When they looked out over the city walls they found that the Greeks had all gone and the ships had gone too. The Trojans thought that they must have finally given up and gone home. But in the distance, on one of the sand dunes, a strange object was seen and it seemed to be moving closer to the city. The Trojans sent out a party of men to investigate but they never returned! That night, all that could be heard in the darkness was an ominous grinding, roaring sound as something seemed to draw nearer to the city. The next morning they were met with an even stranger sight than the night before. Outside the city was what appeared to be a huge horse standing before the city gates. What was it? Why was it there?

The people of Troy could talk of nothing else. Some thought it was a monster come to destroy them. Some thought it was just a giant horse made of wood. Others thought it was a gift from the gods and a few thought it was a trap set by the Greeks. 'But are you saying the entire Greek army is hiding inside?' people said to these few. 'Don't be ridiculous!' They had added, 'Anyway there are no doors on it.' The priests decided that it was a gift from the Greeks to the gods and that therefore they must take it into the city to honour the gods or else they would anger them and that could lead to the destruction of the city.

The king of Troy, Priam, couldn't decide what to do, so he summoned all his royal advisors and had each of them tell him what they thought he should do. After hearing all their advice, in the end the King decided to follow the advice of his priests.

At the break of the next day the people of Troy brought the great horse into the city. The next thing they did was to celebrate the end of the war and the defeat of the Greeks, making sure that they honoured the gods with *sacrifices. They danced and they drank and they ate and they sang until eventually they all lay asleep and exhausted on the floors and tables of the city.*

Once the city was silent, something stirred from within the horse. Odysseus' plan was not to hide the entire army inside the horse, as that would have been impossible, but to hide just ten of the best soldiers in the Greek army, Odysseus being among them. Underneath the belly of the horse a secret trap door swung open and a rope dropped down. The ten Greeks then descended on the rope led by Odysseus. Of course, they would not have been able to fight all the Trojans themselves, but Odysseus' plan was not to fight anyone quite yet. He crept over the sleeping Trojans and made his way to the city gates. He and his men then unlocked the gates and swung them open. And this is where the second part of Odysseus' plan came in. Odysseus had ordered the rest of the Greeks to sail back towards Greece but not to sail all the way back, just as far as was necessary so that they would vanish behind the horizon. Then they were to wait until dark before returning to Troy. When Odysseus and his men opened the gate, waiting on the other side was the Greek army. They charged in and it didn't take them long to capture and kill the Trojans and so finally win the war against Troy. That day Odysseus was hailed a hero of the Greeks and, as you have heard today, the story of his plan and the Greek victory over the Trojans is still being told. And today there is a very famous saying that comes from this story: 'Beware of Greeks bearing gifts!'[1]

The Greeks had won and Helen was retrieved. After ten long years it was finally time for the Greeks to return home. Odysseus stood before his men and told them that they were now able to return to their families. They cheered and took their positions in all of Odysseus' 12 ships ready for the journey home. Odysseus was as anxious about the journey home as he was about the war itself.

Alternative PhiE session: philosophy of beauty

> TQ: Was Helen the most beautiful woman in the world?

---

1   This modern phrase derives from Virgil's Aeneid (Book 2): 'Do not trust the horse, Trojans. Whatever it is, I fear the Greeks even when they bring gifts.'

Nested Questions

- What makes someone beautiful?
- How do people decide what is beautiful?
- Can something be 'the most beautiful'?
- Socratic Question: What is beauty?

Extension Activity: Eratosthenes and the round Earth

TQ: How were the Greeks able to hide their ships behind the horizon?

This question could be used to run an enquiry related to the topic of Earth, Sun and Moon as the answer lies in the Earth's roundness.

It was a Greek who first suggested that the Earth was not flat but round. His name was Eratosthenes (circa 276–195 BCE) and he was able to work this out by comparing the differing angles of sunbeams in relation to the ground. (TQ: How would this prove that the Earth is round?) Among other things, Eratosthenes is also thought to have invented the subject of Geography and to have estimated the circumference of the Earth with surprising accuracy.

The Battle (The Ciconians)

Philosophy

This story is one of the most intriguing of the stories of the *Odyssey*, and, together with The Laestrygonians, is seldom included in versions of the *Odyssey* for young people. I think one reason for this is that The Ciconians can be seen to reflect a very different set of values from those of modern Western societies. It was quite normal for the Greeks to have no qualms about taking slaves, slaughtering an enemy or harbouring an attitude of ill will towards their enemies. Rieu points out, in the Penguin edition of the *Odyssey*, that this was a common attitude until later Christianity. The word 'barbarian', also used by the Romans to distinguish themselves from those not Latinised, comes from the Greek for 'those that are not Greek', or, more accurately, 'those that do not *speak* Greek [well]' (*'barbaroi'* – *'bar-bar'* literally indicating the sound made by non-Greek speakers).

In many situations, it may be appropriate to omit this story with young people, but in a *philosophical* version of the *Odyssey*, I think it appropriate to reintroduce it – and other 'awkward stories' – to older children. The story is an excellent stimulus for thinking about the issues it raises precisely *because* of the different values it may reflect and the controversies it highlights. For instance, it is great for discussing 'the ethics of war' or 'cultural relativism' – the view that 'the truth' for any culture is relative to the values of that culture (see The Laestrygonians on page 69 and its supplementary online section).

The notion of universal human rights emerged from the Enlightenment movement of the 18th century and so its ideas would have been quite alien to the Greeks of Homer's time. Having said all this, Homer's position is far from obvious. Though he has his hero attack a town quite unprompted, the story goes to show dissent and insubordination amongst his crew. And, given that the outcome does not favour the Greeks, it is unclear what Homer's opinion of their actions might have been. This would make an excellent discussion topic for older students.

I have only included The Ciconians with Year 5 and 6 primary age children (age 10 and 11) and older. It is up to you, as the class teacher, whether or not you think this story is appropriate for your class. It works as a good follow-on session from The Wooden Horse and addresses the second of the two questions raised in the previous Chapter's introduction: *What is it right or justifiable to do during a war once you're engaged in one?* (This is the concept of *jus in bello*.)

The 'battle' referred to in the title alludes to the battle between Odysseus and his men as much as to the battle between the Greeks and the Ciconians. And perhaps it could also refer to the 'battle' between old and new values.

Remember to use the correct set of online maps (see page xxii) depending on whether you are going to include this story and The Laestrygonians or not.

Storykit

Names to learn in this story

Ismarus (iss-**ma**-rus): The coast that is the home of the Ciconians.
Ciconians (si-**koe**-neeyuns): Allies of the Trojans during the war.
Maron (**ma**-ron): The Ciconian priest of the temple of Apollo.

Keyword list

- Freak wind to Ismarus.
- Enemies: Kill! Kill! Kill!
- Greeks kill all.
- Odysseus protects Maron.
- Odysseus: 'Let's go!'
- Too much fun.
- Ciconians regather.
- Overwhelmed.
- Run away!
- Escape and losses.

Storykit Hint: One-spot storytelling and movement

Sometimes it is appropriate to move around and to make use of the space you may have, for instance, when you are storytelling with very young children. However, on the whole the best kind of storytelling is done on one spot. Gestures and movement are to be encouraged, but using the 'less-is-more' approach. So, if your character is walking somewhere then 'walk on the spot' to physicalise this but keep the movement(s) small and understated. When you describe events such as the trapdoor opening under the wooden horse in the first story then indicate the opening of a trapdoor with your hands as you say it – or just before (see Storykit Hint: Anticipate on page 41).

Synopsis for The Battle (The Ciconians)

A freak wind brings Odysseus and his men to the coast of Ismarus, the home of the Ciconians. The Ciconians were enemies of the Greeks and allies of the Trojans during the war. The Greeks attack them and take a Ciconian town by surprise. They kill many men and divide the spoils. Odysseus recommends that they leave Ismarus while they still have a chance, but the men don't listen and continue to carouse with wine, women and song. The Ciconians in nearby towns hear about the attack from some escaped survivors. They gather a fighting force and quickly attack the Greeks. It is the Greeks this time that are taken by surprise and overwhelmed. The two sides fight all night but the Greeks eventually have to retreat. Six men from each ship are lost.

Story

Figure 3: Leaving Troy.

Upon leaving the coast of Troy, a freak wind brought the ships to a coast north of Troy – quite the opposite direction to where they had intended to go. The coast was that of Ismarus and the home of the Ciconians, who had been allies of Troy during the war. The men, still in the throes of victory, and wanting to take revenge on the allies of their enemies of the past ten years, stormed the first town they could find. The town was soon overwhelmed by the attacking Greeks, and the fighting men of the town were also overcome and most of them killed. Odysseus made an exception, however: he protected the one called Maron, the priest of Apollo. He also protected Maron's wife and child out of respect for his position. For this act of mercy, Maron gave Odysseus his very special wine – the wine, as you will see, would serve Odysseus well in time.

As was the custom when an enemy town was attacked, the Greeks divided the plunder amongst themselves. Odysseus said that they must leave immediately, and that it would be unwise to stay in Ismarus for too long, but his words fell on deaf ears. He pleaded and argued with his men but they were enjoying themselves too much, and were still intoxicated by yet another victory.

The ethics of war 2 (*jus in bello*)

To help make a smooth segue from the previous session, you may prefer to begin this enquiry with a discussion around the justifications of war. It may be useful to contrast this situation with that of the war against the Trojans, as many may feel that though the war against the Trojans was justified this is not. If you do, make sure you do not allow this discussion to take up too much time as it will likely cover much of the same ground from the PhiE in The Wooden Horse.

> TQ 1: Were Odysseus and his men right to attack the Ciconians?

Nested Questions

- a) Was it *prudent* of them to attack the Ciconians? b) Was it *morally* right of them to attack the Ciconians? (For more on the distinction between prudential and moral goods, see *Appendix 1: The Hero* on page 159. You may want to return to this discussion when you reach The Hero.)
- Is Odysseus' recommendation prudential or moral?
- Is the attack on the Ciconians comparable with the attack on the Trojans?

> TQ 2: Should there be rules in war? If so, what should the rules of war be?

Nested Questions

- How would it be possible to make sure that any rules agreed upon are not being broken during a war?
- Should there be only one injunction: *to win at any cost*? (This makes an excellent stimulus for discussion, particularly for secondary students, presented as follows: 'There should be only one rule in war: *to win at any cost.*' Discuss.)
- Odysseus seems to think that there are certain people among the enemy that should be protected (he protects the priest Maron from his own men). Is he right to think this? If so, who do you think, though they are among the enemy, should be protected and why?
- You may want to introduce the Geneva Convention to the class so that they can explore the contemporary legal/moral issues that emerge from this session.
- a) If a war is legally right, does that mean that it is morally right? b) If a war is morally right does that mean that it is legally right?

Here are some of the suggested conditions that have been made for *jus in bello* (justice in war). Introduce them if, and when, you see fit:

- The war engaged in must not produce more evil than the evil the war was waged to stop. (Question: What is meant by 'evil'?)
- It is not permissible to harm non-combatants and/or civilians. (Question: Are there *any* circumstances when it would be permissible to harm non-combatants and/or civilians?)

Story continued …

Whilst they were drinking the wine, feasting on the food and enjoying the many other rewards of their victory, some surviving Ciconians had escaped to another nearby town. Word quickly spread among the Ciconian people that one of their towns had been attacked by Greeks, so the Ciconians gathered their remaining forces quickly and made their way, full of revenge, towards the celebrating Greeks.

Only a short time later, and complete with bronze spears and chariots, the Ciconians, as numerous as there are flowers in spring, fell upon the sacked town. Odysseus' men were taken utterly by surprise. They never thought the Ciconians would organise themselves so quickly. Except for Odysseus, the Greeks weren't really thinking at all. Many of them still drunk, the Greeks had to fight for their lives. And they fought well all night and into the next day though they were outnumbered. They were soon overwhelmed by the Ciconians, who were gathering greater forces by the hour, as more arrived from inland.

A retreat was coordinated, and Odysseus managed to get his men aboard the ships to make an escape. For their imprudent actions there was a cost, however: they had lost six men from each ship to the Ciconian onslaught. Given that there were 12 ships, it was a lot of men to lose. It was, by all accounts, a lucky escape.

Advanced PhiE: moral relativism

The Ancient Greeks thought that it was okay to kill people that were not Greek.

Suggested Task Questions

TQ 1: If that is what the Ancient Greeks believed, then is it right for them to do this?

TQ 2: Neither we nor modern Greeks believe it is okay to kill people just because they are not of our nationality. So who is right: us or the Ancient Greeks?

TQ 3a: Do you think it would it be okay to kill those that are not Greeks if *you* were an Ancient Greek?

TQ 3b: If you did think it was okay, would you be right to think that?

See online supplement for Chapter 6 for more on moral relativism.

Happiness and Forgetting (The Lotus Eaters) 3

Philosophy

> All you need is happiness ... but not just your own happiness, the happiness of others too. (Marco, 8-year-old boy)

In this session I introduce 'the philosophers of happiness'. Aristotle (384–322 BCE) thought that happiness (or more precisely *eudaimonia* – see Chapter 7: Circe and the Pig Men) was the end goal of all human action; Epicurus (341–270 BCE) famously understood human actions in terms of pleasure, though his precise philosophy is often misunderstood and misrepresented; and John Stuart Mill (1806–73) thought that ethics and policy-making should be directed towards 'the greatest happiness of the greatest number'. This underlies the philosophy known as *utilitarianism*. The children are brought to consider the value of happiness and pleasure through this story in which a juice is introduced that makes the drinker always happy and forgetful of their worries. Odysseus has to make a choice whether to drink the juice or not.

Some children will agree that happiness is all that matters. Others will object that there are more important things such as family, and that happiness is not good if it is inappropriate, as one boy said, 'If you drink the juice then you'll be happy even if a tree falls on your head. That's stupid!' The idea of 'appropriate responses' is a very Aristotelian idea and is known as 'the golden mean'.

Objections that there is more to life than your own personal happiness does not necessarily refute the philosophers of happiness, however, and the quote at the top of this section from the 8-year-old boy suggests how the philosophers of happiness may respond. They may indeed see 'happiness' or 'pleasure' as the ultimate end of human actions yet not recommend that Odysseus drink the juice. Consider why you think they may take these two positions before you read on.

Epicurus would put it like this: though the juice would offer Odysseus a short-term pleasure he would get a greater reward if he were to achieve the longer-term pleasure of his goal to reach home, a pleasure that would also include his friends as well as himself. Mill would say that reaching home would result in a greater happiness and of a greater number, because if they drink the juice then only those who do so will be happy, but if they return home to their families then the crew will be happy and, in addition, so will their families. He would also say that the juice would confer only a lower, animal-like pleasure whereas returning home would result in a higher pleasure available only to human beings. Aristotle would object that the pleasure of drinking the juice is a one-dimensional pleasure and so, as such, would not achieve anything close to his conception of happiness: *eudaimonia* (the reflective and rational flourishing of one's potential as a human being).

Storykit

Names to learn in this story

- **Perimedes** (perry-**mee**-dees): A real character from the *Odyssey* and companion of Odysseus but given a more substantial role in this version for narrative/sessional reasons.

Keyword list

- Time to go home.
- Storm.
- Shipwrecked.
- Search party.
- Search party for the search party (and Perimedes).
- Someone's watching!
- The clearing, the search party and the cups.
- More juice!
- Perimedes works out where they are.
- Masks.
- Choice: to drink or not to drink?
- Odysseus makes his choice.
- Hurry back but too late.
- Leave (one ship down).
- Epilogue: one man is lost.
- Water!

Storykit Hint: Anticipate (using movement to pull your listeners through the story)

Following on from 'one-spot-storytelling', another good storytelling tip for movement is to move in anticipation of something. So, if your character is about to draw a sword, then do the action of drawing a sword just before you say, 'he drew his sword'. This helps to pull the audience through the story, engaging their imaginations as they piece together the narrative before you say it out loud. This requires a bit of conscious effort to begin with but soon becomes natural if you persevere.

Synopsis for Happiness and Forgetting (The Lotus Eaters)

They eventually find their way to a densely forested island that is the home of a people who harvest a fruit that grows only on this island. The juice made from the fruit has the quality of making the recipients permanently happy (for as long as the juice is imbibed) and forgetful of their worries. Some of the men fall under the effects of the juice and Odysseus has to make a choice as to whether to drink the juice or not. They narrowly escape the island but lose one ship and one man in the process.

How you begin this story will be slightly different depending on whether you decide to include The Ciconians or not. The story below has been written to follow on from either of the previous stories: The Wooden Horse or The Ciconians.

Story

Not long after they had disembarked, the clouds darkened and the wind lifted and the sea rolled. Before long a storm was raging and this storm seemed to be the wrath of Zeus himself. It raged for days, battering the ships tirelessly. Eventually the ships were washed up on an unknown island, damaged and in need of repair. They were also running low on fresh water, which is very important on any ship out at sea.

The next day Odysseus ordered a small party of men to search the island for inhabitants and fresh water, whilst the rest of the men set to work on repairing the ships. He ordered them to return to the ships by nightfall whatever they may or may not have discovered. Night fell but the men did not return. Odysseus decided that if they had still not returned by morning, then he would take another party himself to look for them.

Morning came and still the men had not returned. Odysseus took up his spear and shield and led a party of men into the forest. Little did he know that spears and shields would be of little defence against what it was they were to encounter on this island.

Among the men hand-picked to accompany him was a man called Perimedes. Odysseus had chosen him first and foremost because Perimedes was a great friend of his, but also because he knew the geography and history of this part of the world like no other man and this was invaluable to Odysseus.

The forest was dense but they were just about able to track the first party into the forest depths following their footprints and the broken undergrowth left in their trail. As soon as they entered the forest they had an unshakable feeling that they were being watched from above. The men saw leaves move and heard the sounds of something in the trees but saw nothing more.

After a few hours of searching they eventually came to a grassy opening in the forest surrounded by taller trees than they had seen up to then. In the middle of the meadow they saw the lost party of men lying on the grass sleeping next to emptied wooden cups. Odysseus immediately went to the sleeping men and kicked them, ordering them on to their feet, but the men seemed almost not to notice him. One woken soldier looked around in bewilderment and reached out for one of the empty cups saying, 'More juice! More juice!'

Perimedes had seen enough. He turned to Odysseus and said, 'I think I know where we are. I have heard talk of this place and until now thought it only a legend born of sailors' imaginations. I believe that we have landed on the island of the Lotus Eaters. The inhabitants of this island harvest the juice of a fruit that grows only here. The juice has the effect of making the drinker infinitely

Figure 4: The lost garrison of men lying on the grass sleeping.

happy but with no thoughts for anything other than where they might get their next cup of juice. They care for nothing else. These men before you, Odysseus, have no memory of their families or their mission, and if they did, they would care nothing for them. Drinking the juice makes you always happy and it has the power to make you forget your worries and everything that makes you unhappy.'

As Perimedes finished his account the men noticed that they were surrounded, on all sides, by people in the trees wearing masks with different kinds of painted faces on them. Below the faces in the trees, on the grass, had been placed more cups filled with the juice. Odysseus ordered two men to collect some cups and bring them to him. Upon seeing the cups the woken soldier cried out, 'Give me that!' Odysseus wanted to see what would happen, so he handed the soldier the cup. He drained it in an instant, the juice running down his face, so eager was he to consume it. Once he had finished it he fell back into the grass with a look of intense satisfaction. Then he stood up and offered another cup to Odysseus himself, saying, 'You must drink this nectar. You will lose all your worries and will be forever happy as the only thing you will desire will be growing all around you plentifully. You will never be unhappy again. Drink!' he urged. 'Drink!'

Odysseus held the drink to his nose and sniffed; a wave of pleasure surged through him. He had to decide whether to drink the juice or not.

The value of happiness

> TQ: Should Odysseus drink the juice or not?

Nested Questions

- If you could be happy all the time and forget all your worries, would that be a good thing?
- Is happiness the most important thing?
- Is there anything more important than happiness?
- Socratic Question: What is happiness?

You could choose to run an enquiry on the Task Question but you may find that they fall on one side of the debate because of their narrative investment (i.e. they will want Odysseus to get home). If you find that they are tending towards unanimity then you may choose to run a 'split debate' (see page 20). Alternatively, follow these steps:

1 *For and against*: Give the class two minutes or so to think of as many reasons as they can why he *should* drink the juice. Follow this by giving them another two minutes to think of as many reasons as they can why he *shouldn't* drink the juice. Do step one using the Talk Time model in pairs or groups (see page 4).

2 *Role-play*: Split the class into two equal halves and ask one side of the class to role-play 'Perimedes' and to argue that they should not drink the juice. The other half of the class should role-play 'the soldier' who has recommended that Odysseus drink the juice, and they should try to persuade 'Odysseus' that he should drink the juice. Allow one child from each side to make their case, either by constructing an argument of their own, or by responding to someone from the other side. Remind them from time to time that they are role-playing and so should stay in character.

3 *Make-up-your-mind time*: First of all, ask them to role-play Odysseus and to make the decision whether to drink the juice or not on his behalf. The next step is to explain that the children will no longer be role-playing but will have to *decide for themselves* what they think about Odysseus' decision: do they think he should drink the juice or not? Try to identify who in the classroom, if anyone, thinks that he should drink the juice and find out why they think so. If they think he should drink the juice because he will always be happy and/or that happiness is the most important thing in our lives, then you may be able to use their insight to segue into the next step.

4 *The philosophers of happiness*: If you don't have an insight from the children to introduce this step then introduce it anyway. Explain that there were some philosophers who thought that happiness is the most important thing in our lives. Ask them if they agree with those philosophers, but most importantly, ask them to say why they agree or disagree with 'the philosophers of happiness'. It is up to you whether you introduce any of the philosophers mentioned in the teacher's introduction to this chapter. For older children this may be appropriate but for the younger ones just saying that *there are* philosophers who thought that happiness is the most important thing in our lives should be enough to engage them.

Story continued ...

Though he was tempted to drink the juice, Odysseus thought about his wife and son and about how important to him it was to see them again, and, with this thought, he tossed the cup away. Perimedes and the other men followed his example. They threw the other men over their shoulders and ran back to the ships as fast as they could. When they eventually reached them they saw, on the beach next to the ships, some more of the wooden cups they had seen in the forest clearing ... and they were empty! 'We may already be too late!' said Perimedes.

They discovered that, fortunately, *only some of the men had drunk the juice, but,* unfortunately, *those that had not were too few to be able to man all 12 ships. They were going to have to leave one ship behind. They took all the men who had drunk the juice and tied them up below the decks, then they cast off and set sail as quickly as they could.*

Four days later, the men below deck were still desperate to get more juice and had only said these words the entire time: 'More juice! Must have more juice!' On the fifth day, Odysseus checked the men again, as he had every day, and they seemed calm, so he released just one man to make sure. The man waited until he was free and then ran for the deck hurling himself over the edge of the ship shouting, 'More juice! More juice!' He swam out into the open ocean repeating this mantra until he could be heard no more. Odysseus kept the men tied up for another two days before he decided they were well enough to be released.

They still had not found any fresh water, and they were becoming desperate. Odysseus said to Perimedes, 'We are like the men who drank the juice: we are just as dependent on water!' He ordered the lookout to let him know the moment he had sighted land.

Extension Activity: pleasure and pain

There was once a philosopher in Ancient Greece called Epicurus who thought that pleasure was the most important thing. However, there was a German philosopher much later on called Friedrich Nietzsche (1844–1900) who thought very differently. He thought that pain and difficulty were just as important, if not more important, than pleasure.

> TQ: Who do you agree with on this issue and why?

4 Nobody's Home (The Cyclops)

Philosophy

At first glance, this story appears to be the least yielding when it comes to finding philosophy for discussion. But take a closer look and the philosophy starts to *materialise from nothing*. I say 'materialise from nothing' because I have found the most successful philosophical discussion emerging from this session to be about *non-existent entities*. This topic emerges from both the content of the story (i.e. his use of the word 'nobody' to trick the Cyclops – 'nobody' seeming to be a referring term for someone that isn't there) and a feature of the story (i.e. that it contains a famous mythical creature – mythical creatures being perfect examples of non-existent entities).

So, how can something that doesn't exist have certain qualities or features? Does our collective reference to a Cyclops somehow give it existence, perhaps in our minds, in our culture, or in some other way? Some philosophers have thought so. If so, what kind of existence would this be? It's certainly not the kind of existence something like a rabbit has. Or is it simply *that a Cyclops does not exist in any way*? But if this is the case, how can you meaningfully speak about one – how can you tell the story you are about to tell?

Note: This story contains a clear example of a key Ancient Greek theme and one that runs throughout the *Odyssey*: *hubris*, 'downfall brought about by excessive pride'. Odysseus' announcement revealing his true identity to Polyphemus from the prow of his ship endangers both himself and his crew by inciting the wrath of the god Poseidon no less. It would, however, take another act of hubris to seal the ship's ultimate fate: that of the character Eurylochus when he makes his subversive speeches to the crew on Thrinacia (see The Cattle of Helios on page 115), adding Helios to the list of angry gods intent on destroying them. The concept of hubris will play an important role when discussing whether Odysseus was a hero or not (see The Hero in Appendix 1).

Storykit
Names to learn in this story

- **Polyphemus** (polly-**fe**-mus): One of a race of Cyclopes and the son of the god Poseidon.
- **Poseidon** (pu-**si**-dun): God of the sea, and one of the most important of the Olympian gods. He wields a trident.

Keyword list

- Beached.
- Morning: explore for help (wine).
- Cave.
- Cheese.
- Owner returns: Cyclops (plus tree).
- Make friends – make lunch!
- Trapped.
- Cyclops goes out (snacks first!).
- What to do?
- Returns with sheep and goes out in the morning (after breakfasting!).
- Plan: stake.
- Returns with sheep (snacks again!).
- Wine and 'Nobody' (plus gift).
- Stake in the eye.
- More Cyclopes (Polyphemus).
- Nobody trick.
- Still trapped.
- Another plan.
- Out with the sheep.
- Last ram and out.
- Run away!
- Nobodeeeeey!
- The getaway.
- Proud.
- Announcement and revenge (Poseidon).
- Rock.
- Second rock.
- Sinking.
- Finally safe but only just.

Storykit Hint: Memorising stories

This is one of the longest stories in the *Odyssey* to memorise but unfortunately it happens near the beginning of the epic, so you'll need to have a go at memorising a longer story sooner rather than later to tell this in its proper place. Here are some memorisation hints and tips:

- Read the story through several times and *read actively*. That is to say, don't read in that lazy way we are accustomed to do when reading for pleasure. Read it *out loud* and let the images formulate fully in your mind before reading on.
- On the second or third reading, make your own *Keyword list*. It is better to make your own list because it helps you to process the information more thoroughly and you will choose the words that are best for *you* to help recall the story.
- Visualise the events of the story in your mind so that you are simply describing 'what you see' rather than trying to remember a long list of words. (See Storykit Hint: Visualisation and confidence building on page 77.)
- Causally link the sequence of events. They are shipwrecked (The Lotus Eaters), so what do they need to do? This should jog your memory about what comes next: 'Oh yeah,' you say to yourself, 'they will need to repair the ships and seek for help because they're low on water.' This should lead you naturally to the forest scene (what do they find?), which leads to the clearing scene etc. If you try to remember a series of isolated events then memorisation is much harder, but in stories, *everything happens for a reason*.
- Practise telling the story either on your own when you have a minute (such as when you are on a journey or waiting for a bus, etc.) or tell your children, your spouse, a friend – anyone who'll listen! The more you tell, the easier it is. You will also find that the more stories you learn, the easier learning new stories gets.
- Take *pauses* in your storytelling to take stock. Pausing when you speak is also a very effective way of drawing people into what you are saying. Of course, if you pause too much your telling becomes laborious, but get the balance right, and your telling will be more engaging *and* you will have the benefit of giving yourself time to think.
- Turn your long list of words into easy, bite-size *chunks*. The Cyclops story, for instance, can be reduced to just three things: 1) they explore; 2) they get trapped; 3) they escape – just! Then 1) can be reduced to just three things again: a) they arrive; b) they find the cave; c) the Cyclops returns. Carry on like this 'in threes' as long as necessary. (See online for more synopses 'in threes'.)

Synopsis for Nobody's Home (The Cyclops)

They find another island and on it a cave that belongs to a Cyclops (Polyphemus) who traps them in the cave and begins to eat the crew. Eventually, Odysseus devises a plan to escape by getting the Cyclops drunk and telling the Cyclops that his (Odysseus') name is 'Nobody'. While asleep after getting him drunk, the men blind the Cyclops with a giant stake. They are kept safe from the other Cyclopes who come to find out what all the shouting is about. Polyphemus blames 'Nobody' for the injury! Still trapped inside the cave, they escape by strapping themselves under the Cyclops' sheep. Polyphemus discovers that they have escaped before they get away from the island. Odysseus taunts the Cyclops from the safety of his ship but the Cyclops destroys another ship by throwing rocks in their general direction. This is where Odysseus makes an enemy of Poseidon, who turns out to be Polyphemus' father.

Story

In this story I want you to imagine that you are one of Odysseus' crew.

Having left the island of the Lotus Eaters, no land is sighted for many days. There is one night when the clouds are so thick that there is no light from the moon or the stars and the ship floats aimlessly through the water. In the darkness the ships suddenly come to a halt as they run aground on some unseen beach. It is only when morning comes that you are able to see where it is the gods have brought you.

When dawn arrives you see that you have been delivered to the shores of another island. It is mountainous and barren with rocky crags all over it. There are sheep and goats grazing on the grass that grows around the rocks and coats the hillsides, but they are no ordinary sheep or goats. They are huge and closer in size to a large cow. There's nothing for it but to explore the island and hope that you find someone civilised and able to help. Fresh water is what you most need.

Odysseus takes with him a party of twelve men to explore the island. You are among the 12. In the event that you find an inhabitant of this wild land, Odysseus takes with him several wineskins of his best and strongest wine as a gift for anyone you may meet. It's the wine that Maron gave him in thanks for Odysseus' protection of Maron and his family. The rest of the crew are ordered to herd as many sheep and goats as they can for food to be stored on each ship.

Many hours you spend roaming the island but there are no signs of life or civilisation. You are just about to give up and return to the ships when one of you notices, at the top of a slope of loose rock, a cave mouth with signs of life outside it!

Looking up, you notice, outside the cave, a huge basket tied to a tree growing over the top of the entrance. There are also bunches of dried herbs tied together around the cave.

You venture up the slope and enter the cave to find out who might live there. Inside you find that nobody's home. But there's plenty of evidence that this is somebody's home. There is a bed and a table and chair, but they are not like furniture you have seen before. They are huge. Whoever owns these must himself be the size of a tower. Going further into the cave you notice that there is a pen at the back where animals must be kept, though it is empty now. And in another far corner there is a stack of homemade goat's cheese with some bread and milk. You are all starving and forget yourselves as you tuck into the food.

So busy are you eating that you only hear the sound of giant footsteps approaching the cave when it is too late. A huge shadow blocks out the light from the entrance as the cave's owner returns home. You turn to look and what you see fills you with horror. Your way out is barred by the figure of a gigantic man wearing a tunic of goat's skins and holding a full-sized tree trunk at his side in one hand. But the most terrifying thing about this giant is that he is looking at you through one, single, blinking eye in the centre of his forehead.

He is a Cyclops: a race of lawless, one-eyed giants that inhabit these lands that you have only ever heard of in stories.

Odysseus steps forward and explains that you are shipwrecked and in need of the help of a host. He also tells the giant that you have brought him gifts. 'You are fools to come here, but you have indeed brought me gifts – yourselves!' replies

Figure 5: You turn to look and what you see fills you with horror.

the Cyclops as he reaches forward and picks up one of the men that stand before him (fortunately, it isn't you!) and he pops him into his mouth and eats him in just two mouthfuls, crunching the bones up before washing your shipmate down with some goat's milk. He then rolls a huge boulder across the entrance as if it was nothing more than a toy. He sits down, burps, farts and falls into a noisy sleep. You are now trapped in the cave with this man-eating monster. One of the party says, 'Let us kill him now with our spears while he sleeps.' But Odysseus reminds you that if you kill him then you would also seal your own fate as there would be no one able to remove the boulder.

After the Cyclops has rested, he gets up and rolls the boulder to one side, then leaves and rolls it back again, keeping you all trapped inside while he gets on with his daily chores. 'What are we going to do?' one of the party says to Odysseus. 'If we don't get out of here soon, we will all end up in the belly of that thing!' 'I know,' replies Odysseus. 'Now, let me think.'

A short time later the Cyclops returns and brings with him his sheep and goats to be safely penned in at the back of the cave for the night. He rolls the boulder back to close off the way out, then he takes another couple of men for supper (fortunately, not you this time, but if you don't get out soon it will be). Again, he washes them down with milk before falling asleep.

Once the Cyclops has left the next morning to shepherd his herds (and not before he devours another two men for breakfast!) Odysseus announces that he has a plan. He instructs the remainder of you to chisel the tree that the Cyclops brought with him so that it has a sharp point at one end, like a giant pencil. You practise lifting and charging your giant spear, then you place it to one side and hope that the Cyclops doesn't notice how it has changed.

When he returns for the night with his sheep and goats and eats another crew member, Odysseus steps forward once more and this time offers the Cyclops some of Maron's wine he had brought with him. The Cyclops tries it and finds it to be very pleasing indeed.

'This is good,' says the Cyclops. 'Give me more! And tell me your name as I would like to offer you a gift of my own in return.' Odysseus hands the giant some more wine and he drinks it all down in one go this time.

'My name – in answer to your question – is "Nobody",' says Odysseus. 'A strange name,' muses the Cyclops. 'Well, No-bo-dy, I would like to give you a gift in return for the delicious wine you have given me. My gift is ... that I shall eat you last!' And with that he laughs.

Despite hearing this, Odysseus laughs with him and continues to chat amicably with the Cyclops, offering him more and more wine with each exchange. Slowly, and without noticing, the Cyclops becomes drunk. His words

Figure 6: Slowly, and without noticing, the Cyclops becomes drunk.

begin to slur and his huge eyelid gets heavier and heavier until eventually he says to Odysseus with words that are barely distinguishable, 'I like you ... you're my best friend, you are ...'. And with that he falls over, landing on his chest with a thunderous crash, his neck twisted and his face to one side.

'Now!' hisses Odysseus, and you all lift the wooden stake with your combined might. You aim the tree trunk, and then charge towards the sleeping eye of the Cyclops. It makes an almighty crunching sound as the giant stake impales the huge eye. The Cyclops immediately wakes up screaming, clutching the stake that protrudes from his eye. With one pull he rips it out and screams even louder than before. Racked with pain and anger, he swings his huge arms to-and-fro to try to find you, and you have to duck down to avoid being thrown against the wall.

All the noise has attracted the attention of the other Cyclopes that live in caves nearby. Now, you can just about deal with one Cyclops when it is blinded, but you couldn't possibly deal with a host of sighted Cyclopes. You hear what must be the footsteps of at least a dozen Cyclopes ascending the slope and you all freeze with terror. When they reach the boulder, however, one of them shouts in from outside.

'What's going on in there, Polyphemus? What's all the noise for? Are you being robbed?'

'I've been blinded and tricked,' screams the injured Cyclops who you now realise is called 'Polyphemus'.

'Who has wronged you?' the other Cyclops shouts back.

'NOBODY has blinded me and NOBODY has tricked me and NOBODY is here now, though I can't find him!' shouts Polyphemus full of anger.

'Nobody is in there? No wonder you can't find him!' The other Cyclopes look at each other and guess that Polyphemus must have been drinking again. 'If there's nobody there, then there's nobody to be afraid of and nothing to worry about, Polyphemus. Now go back to bed!' And, with that, they wander off and return to their business, leaving Polyphemus to his moaning and his pain.

After that narrow escape, you now have the blinded, angry Cyclops to worry about. He eventually calms down and sits on his bed. He manages to find a bowl into which he puts some water and, using a rag, he nurses his wound. You have to remain absolutely silent and still to avoid being detected. You can barely breathe.

You endure a very uncomfortable night, Odysseus occasionally whispering to you about the next part of the plan only when Polyphemus is fast asleep and snoring. The next morning the Cyclops has to release his livestock but he is worried that you will escape if he rolls the boulder too far. He might be stupid but he's not that stupid!

He rolls the boulder just far enough to allow one of his livestock through and, as each goat or sheep is let out, he checks its back and sides by feeling with his big hands, to see if any of you are trying to hide on them. But none of you are hiding on the backs and sides of the sheep and goats – you are hiding underneath them, tied to their bellies. It might be smelly and dirty under there, but it's better than being eaten alive!

Once all the crew are through, there is only one animal left: a full-grown ram, the best of the flock, and under its belly is Odysseus. As Polyphemus feels the ram he says to it, 'Why are you the last to leave today? Normally, you are first out.' He checks the ram again. For a minute you think that Polyphemus has suspected your trickery and seen through your plan. But then he says, 'It must be because you are grieving for your master's eye.' With his massive hand he urges the ram through the gap and out of the cave. He quickly rolls the boulder back to imprison you once more but without knowing that he has, in fact, secured your escape.

'We must run as fast as we can to warn the others and get away from this island, because the moment he finds out he's been tricked, he will not be happy,' says Odysseus as you all climb out from under your animals and brush yourselves down. When you are about halfway back to the ships you hear an almighty roar: 'NOBODEEEEEEEEY!' Polyphemus must have found out that you have escaped.

Figure 7: It might be smelly and dirty under there, but it's better than being eaten alive!

As you run on to the beach you shout to the other men to get into the ships and cast off immediately. You have to leave many things behind on the beach – there just isn't time to collect anything. Just as the ships cast off, Polyphemus comes stumbling onto the beach saying, 'Nobody's here, I can smell him!' Of course, being blinded he can't see you, so, as quietly as you can, you row for your lives away from the cursed shores of this island.

Odysseus has many qualities: he is resourceful (in Ancient Greek the word for 'nobody' is me tis, but if you run the two words together, metis becomes the Greek for 'resourceful'), he is cunning and clever, as you have already seen in previous adventures. But he is also proud.

When he believes the ships to be at a far enough distance from the shore, Odysseus stands on the prow of his ship and shouts out to the Cyclops: 'Polyphemus, you will recognise this as the voice of "Nobody", only I am not really "Nobody": I am Odysseus, son of Laertes and King of Ithaca. It is

Figure 8: I am Polyphemus, son of *Poseidon*, the Earth-shaker, and he will hear my plea and have me avenged!

Odysseus who today tricked you, it is Odysseus who today blinded you and it is Odysseus who stands here having escaped your clutches to taunt you from the safety of his ship.'

Even from this distance you can see Polyphemus' rage as he shouts back across the water: 'I am Polyphemus, son of Poseidon, the Earth-shaker, and he *will hear my plea and have me avenged!' He then reaches out to a pinnacle of rock that he tears from its top and throws with all his might towards the sound of Odysseus' voice.*

The rock plunges into the sea next to Odysseus' ship and the ship is rocked from side to side like a child's bath toy. Some men fall into the sea and Odysseus orders the ships to turn around and retreat to the ocean. But by now Polyphemus is searching the beach for another rock to launch at the ships. It is not long before he finds one. This rock finds a target. The rock makes a hole directly in the middle of one of the ships and it starts to sink. The crew of the remaining ships save as many men as possible whilst a shower of boulders threatens to sink them all. But in the end the danger is too pressing and some men have to be left behind. Once out of range from Polyphemus' throw you are finally safe. You sail on with heavy hearts for the men that were lost but grateful for your own narrow escape.

Non-existent entities

Explain the following to the class:

A Cyclops is an example of a mythical creature. Imagine two children are arguing in the playground about how many eyes a Cyclops has. They can't agree on the number of eyes a Cyclops has.

> TQ 1: How many eyes *does* a Cyclops have?

If you feel they need some help here, then simply add that one of the children thinks that a Cyclops has one eye 'because everyone knows that they do!' The other child, on the other hand, says, 'They can have as many eyes as you want, because they're not real.'

Nested Questions

- How can something that isn't real have one eye (or, for that matter, *any* eyes)?
- Do mythical creatures exist?
- How many eyes does a Cyclops have if it doesn't exist?

- How many eyes does a Cyclops have if it does exist?
- If a Cyclops was born with the deformity of having two eyes, would it still be a Cyclops?
- The Ancient Greeks thought that unicorns were real, only very difficult to find. Does that mean that, for the Ancient Greeks, unicorns were real?
- Socratic Question: What is real?
- If 'cyclops' means 'one-eyed' then does that mean that Cyclopes only have one eye?
- Does a cartoon character, such as 'Bart' from *The Simpsons*, exist?
- Presumably, Bart had a mother, and she must have had a mother, Bart's grandmother and she too must have had a mother, and so on. Does Bart's great-great-great-great-grandmother exist?

An exercise to help bring out the controversy

Take two pieces of A4 paper and on one of them write: 'A Cyclops has one eye.' On the other write: 'A Cyclops isn't real.' Put both pieces of paper on the floor in the centre of the room so that all the children can see. Then ask the following Task Question.

> TQ 2: Can both sentences be true at the same time?

What about these pairs of sentences?

- 'Polyphemus is a Cyclops.' and 'Polyphemus has two eyes.'
- 'Polyphemus has one eye.' and 'Polyphemus has two eyes.'
- 'Polyphemus is a Cyclops.' and 'Polyphemus is a giant.'
- 'Polyphemus is a Cyclops.' and 'Polyphemus has only three fingers on each hand.'
- 'Polyphemus is a Cyclops.' and 'Polyphemus is a unicorn.'

Extension Activity: lawlessness

The *Odyssey* tells us that the Cyclopes are a lawless race of shepherds. This provides an opportunity for a discussion on the implications of living in a lawless society.

Suggested Task Questions

TQ 1: What would it be like to live in a lawless society?

TQ 2: Would it be good to live in a society where there are no rules?

TQ 3: Could you have a society that had only one rule: 'No rules!'?

TQ 4: Would it be good (or even possible) to live in a society where all the inhabitants could do exactly what they wanted?

Captain or Crew? (Aeolus and the Bag of Winds)

5

Philosophy

This story has an uncanny parallel with a story that Plato told in *The Republic*. Using the image of a ship, he asks us to consider who is best placed to be captain: the half-blind and ignorant ship-owner, the crew who have no understanding of navigation, or someone skilled in the art of navigation? Using this simile, Plato launches his famous critique of democracy – the form of government at the time in Greece. And although the democracy of Ancient Greece was a version very different from that of our own (in that it did not include, as eligible voters, women or slaves, only Greek, male citizens), his criticisms are still relevant today. To what extent should those without the necessary education, skills and knowledge, that is, 'the people', play a part in the way we are governed? It is often taken for granted that democracy is the best and right way for governments to function, but it can also be healthy for us to step back sometimes to consider this position critically, even if it helps us to clarify in our own minds why, though democracy may be deficient, it may be the best system of government open to us. As Winston Churchill famously said, 'It has been said that democracy is the worst form of government except all the others that have been tried.'

Asking these questions may also help us to think about how we may improve our prized democratic system if we don't decide that there's a better system in the process. This story offers a wonderful opportunity to introduce a discussion of political philosophy to the children. The questions to bear in mind when pursuing these kinds of discussion are 'Who should rule?' and 'Who should decide?'[1] The children may well spot the 'deliberate mistake' that democracy is presupposed in that they vote *democratically* to decide whether to follow democracy or not! They are then brought to a logical problem of political philosophy: *how do you decide what kind of rule there should be without presupposing it?*

---

1   This summary of the questions of political philosophy comes from Jonathan Wolff's *Introduction to Political Philosophy* (Oxford)

Storykit
Names to learn in this story

- **Aeolus** (a-**o**-lus): Keeper of the winds.
- **Polus** (**poe**-lus): Invented for this version.

Keyword list

- 'Land ... *I think*!'
- Island of bronze.
- Invited guests.
- Water and rest at last.
- The gift and a rumour.
- Depart and promise.
- Ninth day: home!
- Sleep and argument.
- Autocracy or democracy?
- The vote is cast.
- The bag is untied.
- Storm released.
- Lost again.
- Promise.

Storykit Hint: Describing your story and building an atmosphere

Some of the stories in the original *Odyssey* are remarkably short and devoid of description and atmosphere while others are given a great deal of both or, in some cases, are overburdened with detail. Whatever the reasons for this and whatever audiences 3,000 years ago expected, there's a lot we can do to improve the balance of description, atmosphere and detail for today's younger audiences.

Set the scene: It is important to describe the scenes with enough detail for them to be able to imagine the scene well but without too much detail that they lose interest. Do this whenever there is a change of scene but keep your description to what is necessary.

Provide clues: Everything in a story should be there for a reason. Describing the cave of the Cyclops with its huge furniture gives the audience some information about the owner: whoever they are, they're huge! The pen that you describe houses the animals that will play a crucial role in the men's escape, and the food they find is the motivation for them to act imprudently so that they get trapped. You should not spend time describing features that will play no role other than to build an atmosphere, and this should be done sparingly as you should never lose sight of the plot. However, though the plot is important, if you simply enumerate the events of the story you are not storytelling. I once set a class the task of telling the stories of the *Odyssey* to someone at home. When I had finished the stories I asked them if anyone had told the stories. One of the children said, 'Well, I didn't really *tell* the stories, I just said what happened.' He had made a distinction between 'saying the plot' (usually 'and then x, and then y and then z happened') and *storytelling*, a large part of which is getting the balance right between plot and description.

Some choice moments in the *Odyssey*, where description can help to build an atmosphere or provide clues, are:

- As the men enter the forest during The Lotus Eaters and their awareness of being watched.
- The cave of the Cyclops.
- The description of the coast of Ithaca when they reach home but just before they are blown back out to sea in Aeolus.
- The cliff-encircled harbour in The Laestrygonians.
- The summoning of the dead in The Underworld.
- The engulfing sea-mist as they approach the island of the Sirens.

Thoughts and feelings: Occasionally you can describe the thoughts and feelings of characters, letting your audience into the character's internal world: for instance, Odysseus' regret at having not told the crew of Scylla. You can also hint at these rather than fully reveal them, as for instance with Circe and Kalypso when intimating their feelings for Odysseus.

Synopsis for Captain or Crew? (Aeolus and the Bag of Winds)

This time they are taken in by Aeolus, the owner of the next island that they find. The men rest and Odysseus is given a gift by Aeolus: a tied, leather bag. A rumour circulates amongst the crew that it contains gold and silver when in fact it contains the imprisoned storm winds that might otherwise hamper their return home. As they return home, an argument breaks out among the crew while Odysseus is sleeping. Just as they reach Ithaca, the bag is opened by the mutinous crew and the winds are released, blowing the ships back out to sea to be lost again. During the storm all but one of the ships are lost.

Story

Again, imagine that you are one of the crew. Now desperate for fresh water, you sail aimlessly on. So in need of water are you that you are becoming delirious and are beginning to see islands where there are none. A few days into your thirsty search the lookout cries, 'Land ahoy! ... I think ...'

Unsure whether this is just another hallucination, you all strain your eyes to see what it is that has puzzled the lookout. A small dot in the distance gradually grows in size as you approach, but as it becomes clearer it also becomes apparent that this is no ordinary island.

A great wall of bronze encircles what you guess must be an island within. It appears, however, impenetrable. As your ships come to a halt before the walled dwelling, a small gate opens at the base of the fortress and a boat emerges. It appears to be a scout-boat and it makes its way towards Odysseus' ship, which is nearest the island.

Odysseus speaks to the men in the boat and it quickly becomes apparent that the exchange is friendly. The boat eventually returns to the island and Odysseus gives the signal to follow. Your ships will never fit through the small aperture in the wall, but no matter because as you near the wall, a much larger, double-doored gate parts to allow your ships' passage.

Odysseus explains that you have arrived at the house of Aeolus, the Keeper of Winds, where he lives with his family of 12, his six daughters and six sons. He further explains that you have all been invited to stay with him a while to recuperate, as his guests. Here, you will feast and rest for as long as necessary. It seems that you have found the sanctuary you so desperately needed, and in the nick of time! As you pass through the gates you see that you have entered a protected paradise.

In all, you remain here for a month. And it is indeed the case that you are able to rest and pass the time relaxing and enjoying the beautiful island. Each night you feast together around a huge table. Odysseus sits at the head of the table beside Aeolus and they talk at great length to each other.

One evening during one of their many conversations, you notice Aeolus give Odysseus a gift. It is a large leather bag tied tightly at the top. Odysseus takes it and thanks him. Over the next few days a rumour begins to circulate amongst the crew. It is speculated that in the bag is a hoard of gold and silver, but it is also rumoured that Odysseus plans not to share this gift with any of you.

The day comes for you to leave. You are all well rested and the ships are fully stocked with food and fresh water. Odysseus and Perimedes, the ship's navigator, have studied and memorised the charts of the surrounding seas and islands that

Figure 9: It is a large leather bag tied tightly at the top.

are in Aeolus' possession, and they have plotted a course home. Perimedes has estimated that you shall reach your homeland of Ithaca in no more than nine days. Odysseus himself promises to sail the ships there personally and vows not to sleep until he has honoured his promise. The thought that you may see your families again in such a short time fills your hearts with warmth and joy.

As you sail and as each day passes, the rumour of the gold and silver in the bag that Aeolus gave to Odysseus does not go away. In fact, it gets worse. When Odysseus is not within earshot, the men talk of it more each day.

The ninth day arrives and, as predicted, a familiar coastline materialises over the horizon. It is the coastline that will lead you back to Ithaca at long last! Odysseus addresses all of you: 'We have come a long way indeed. Here is our home – you can see it with your own eyes. I have not slept, however, for nine days now and I am exhausted. I will need my energy for the celebrations that lie ahead so I am going to sleep awhile. Do not wake me until we reach our treasured shores. And do not lose sight of the coast. We should be home in just a few hours.' With that, Odysseus retires below deck.

Once he has fallen asleep, an argument breaks out amongst the men. It concerns the rumour that has been spreading regarding the bag of gold and silver. The argument is about whether or not to take the bag and open it while Odysseus sleeps. Eventually, the crew splits into two. Two senior members of the crew seem to have become the spokesmen for the two sides of the argument.

Perimedes represents the part of the crew that think they should trust Odysseus to decide what's best. But someone called Polus has been arguing that it is not fair that Odysseus gets to keep the treasure when all the men have endured just as much as he.

The argument slowly turns into an argument about how the ship should be ruled. Perimedes says that it is better to have a captain to rule over the men and make decisions on their behalf (what the Greeks called an autocracy*), while Polus argues that the people of the ship should rule themselves and that it is wrong for the people to be ruled by one man (this the Greeks called a* democracy*).*

Political rule

This makes use of the *debate* strategy described in The Lotus Eaters, but makes it more formal. As this session introduces the children to political philosophy, it is a good session to introduce them also to a simplified version of the parliamentary system. In The Lotus Eaters I said that the children have a stake in certain outcomes for narrative reasons, for example, they wanted Odysseus not to drink the juice because they wanted him to get back home. This story has a conflict of interests. On the one hand, they will want to side with Perimedes because he represents the interests of the hero of the story, but on the other hand, it is Polus who holds the position that is favourable to our modern political sensibilities (i.e. democratic ones).

I have noticed, however, that children do not necessarily share our prejudices in favour of democracy – the classes I have witnessed do not on the whole argue for the democratic position. I have also noticed that this can change if you tell them that we live in a democratic system. It may surprise you to know that many children in primary school do not know this already and if you ask them whether they think we live in a democracy or an autocracy they will often say an autocracy because they perceive our Prime Minister as one man ruling over everyone else – an understandable misconception. If you want to extend this session to a discussion about the merits and demerits of our own political system, certainly with older children, then I suggest you split the discussion into 1) an 'in the story' discussion (*Should the ship be ruled by the crew or by Odysseus?*); and 2) an 'out of the story' discussion (*Should we be ruled democratically as we are, or should be ruled by a King or Queen like we used to be?*). You may prefer to wait for the 'out of the story' discussion to explain our own parliamentary system.

Formal debate

For this activity you will need:

- A gavel – some kind of hammer-device for banging on the table.
- A table – this will act as 'the bench'.
- Voting slips – just cut up lots of scrap paper for them to be able to write one letter on. You will need as many pieces of paper as there are children in the room.
- Pencils – for writing on the voting slip.
- A ballot box – in which to place their filled-in voting slips.

1 Write on the board the two positions – on the left of the board write '(A) Perimedes: The ship should be ruled by a captain (autocracy)' and, on the right-hand side, write '(B) Polus: The ship should be ruled by the people (democracy)'. Explain that *autocracy* and *democracy* are the English words that come from the Greek for these two kinds of rule.

2 Split the class in two to correspond with the two positions on the board, and place a table ('the bench') in between the two halves of the class. Explain that one side of the class shall be arguing for A and the other for B. Some of the children will be disappointed that they can't argue for the position they hold, so explain that they will get a chance to decide which position they will take later, but that in the meantime, they will be engaging in a *debate* and it is important that they learn to think about something from both sides, including the side they don't begin by holding. (Ask them – perhaps afterwards – what reasons there might be for doing this.)

3 Next, give them five minutes or so in their respective groups to come up with reasons to support their position.

4 The two groups then sit opposite each other and take turns to say either: 1) something in *support* of their position; or 2) something in *response* or *reply* to a speaker from the other side. When they speak they have to walk up to 'the bench' to 'address the house'. Have 'a gavel' ready to bang on the table if 'the house' needs 'bringing to order' and allow the children to manage themselves as to who speaks. The rule they should use as a guide is: *if you have already spoken, then you have to wait to see if someone who has not yet spoken wants to contribute; if there is nobody, then you may speak again.* Intervene with the management only if necessary and appeal to their 'maturity' to avoid having to step in.

5 In order to help make the point, explain that because they are not yet arguing for what 'they think', but simply for 'a position', they are not allowed to say 'I think …' at the beginning of their 'reason'. For fun, if they do say 'I think', then they must sit down immediately! This helps to make the point that they are not yet voicing their own opinion. They will find it difficult to speak

without beginning with 'I think ...'. You could suggest the following sentence-starters to help them: 'The ship should be ruled by a captain because ...' or 'The ship should be ruled by the crew because ...'.

6 The next stage of the debate is for them to swap positions. Those that were arguing for A will now argue for B and vice versa. Sometimes it can be a little complicated to remember what side they are arguing for, so, to make life easier, ask them to get up out of their chairs and – literally – swap sides, so they can easily see on the board what their position is. If you have not already told them that this will happen, it often comes as a bit of a surprise, as they have often invested quite a lot in the first position they took. However, its being a surprise can help to make an impression.

7 Make sure that at the end of the debate you leave enough time for them to cast their votes. Make a point of saying that the vote will be 'blind' – that is to say, no one will know who each other voted for (ask them why they think this is done).

8 Give them each a piece of paper and on it they should write either a 'D' for 'democracy' or an 'A' for 'autocracy', depending on which they think is best. Have the meanings of the two words clearly written up on the board. They should then fold the paper and place it in 'the ballot box' (have this ready).

9 Emphasise that they must *think for themselves and make their own decision* based on the reasons they have heard on both sides of the debate. Also remind them that no one will know who voted for what (unless they tell them, of course!).

10 Once the vote has been counted up, the results are announced. Explain that, though this is the result of their classroom-vote on the issue, you will now tell them what happens in the story. Then continue with the next part.

Story continued ...

Eventually a vote is cast. Those that agree with Perimedes stand behind him and those that agree with Polus stand behind Polus until all have taken their places. When it is done, the greater number stands by Polus. The crew have chosen to rule themselves – to become a democracy *aboard their ship. Next, they need to decide whether to take the bag or not. Again, they vote on this as before. The greater number chooses to take the bag and to share its contents out amongst the entire crew equally. Perimedes protests but he is powerless to do anything to stop them and he and his supporters are restrained by some of the other crew members. The bag is taken silently from Odysseus' side. He is not roused – his slumber is deep indeed. The bag is placed on the deck of the ship and Polus unties it.*

Whilst the bag is being untied you notice the familiar shapes of your homes silhouetted along the coast. You are so close that you can see the homely sign of smoke rising from the houses where your families are preparing food, quite unaware that their husbands and fathers are within sight of the shore. But no sooner have you seen your home than it is gone again.

It transpires that inside the bag there is no gold or silver. The rumour was nothing more than … well, a rumour. Aeolus had not given Odysseus a treasury. Instead, being the Keeper of Winds and entrusted with them by the gods, he had given him a bag with the storm winds trapped inside, to ensure Odysseus' – and your – safe return. He had then sent an accompanying breeze to power the ships.

As the storm that has been imprisoned in the bag escapes, all its pent up energy is also released. The ships are corralled into the open ocean once more. The storm rages for days and only gets stronger as it rages. When the storm eventually subsides you are greeted with yet more calamity. Of the ten ships that remained of the 12 that set sail from Troy, only one still sits on top of the water, the others all having been claimed by the violent waves. What's more, you are lost at sea again. The charts that Odysseus and Perimedes viewed at Aeolus' home would only be of use when it is known where you are to start. Now, you could be anywhere.

Polus was among those lost with the other ships. Odysseus seems almost broken with disappointment and betrayal. This being so, he nevertheless turns to the remaining men and he says, 'Men! It is just us now. Whatever it is you have done, my promise to bring you to your homes still holds.'

With great effort, you lift your hearts, take your positions and set sail once more into the unknown.

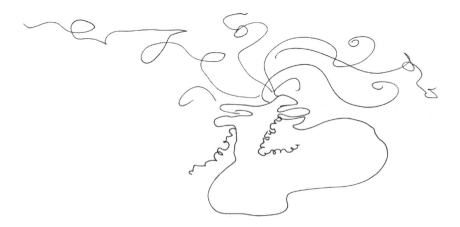

Figure 10: A bag with the storm winds trapped inside.

Extension Activity: punishment, forgiveness and the veil of ignorance

Optional discussion opportunity: Here, you could stop to consider the rights and wrongs of punishment versus forgiveness as regards a leader's role. If you decide not to stop here for a discussion, you could return to this question at a later stage, such as during The Hero session (see Appendix 1). If you decide that you will do this then make a note of it.

A suggested TQ for this could be:

> TQ: Should Odysseus punish his crew or should he forgive them, as he does in the story?
> TQ 2: If he should punish them, then *how* should this be done?

There is enough substance with these two questions for a full session in itself. When (and if) you discuss how Odysseus should punish the crew, I suggest you use a strategy inspired by the American philosopher John Rawls (1921–2002). He thought that in order to reach justice on issues such as this, one needs to apply what he called 'the veil of ignorance'. When asking the children how they think he should punish the crew, tell them that they don't know whether they will be Odysseus (the one giving out the punishment) or one of the crew members (the ones receiving the punishment). Once they have decided what punishment would be right, you could then ask them to flip a coin: heads, they are Odysseus, and tails, they are a crew member. Tell them, before they decide on the punishment, that this will be done. A question worth pursuing is: *Does the veil of ignorance in any way affect their decision? Why?*

Advanced Extension Activity: 'consequentialism'

The view that the goodness of an act is determined by the outcome or consequences is known as *consequentialism*. For many, however, it is not the outcome that determines the goodness of an act but the *intention* of the perpetrator, what the philosopher Kant called a 'goodwill'. For a more advanced discussion with older children, read the following: *The crew decided to have a democracy (that is, for the ship to be ruled by the people). However, things turned out very badly for them.*

Figure 11: The other [ships] all having been claimed by the violent waves.

TQ: If things had turned out well, would that mean that their decision to be democratic would have been a good decision? Or would it still have been a bad decision even though it turned out well?

Nested Questions

- Does the outcome (or *consequences*) of a decision determine its goodness (moral worth)?
- Can a decision be a (morally) good decision even if it turns out badly?
- *'The end justifies the means'*. Is this true?

Dinner Guests (The Laestrygonians) 6

Philosophy

Is it wrong for human beings to eat other human beings? Intuitively, we think that it is, but then, there do seem to be situations where it might be considered permissible. For instance, where – as in the real life situation that the film *Alive* depicts – survival depends on it. Or, as one primary school boy once said, 'It's okay to eat Jesus.' He was referring to the Eucharist, the Catholic version of which includes the principle of *transubstantiation* where the bread and wine is believed to physically change into the body and blood of Christ. There have also been societies of people that have practised cannibalism at different times and places in the world. This raises the interesting question (see online 'When in Rome ...') as to whether cannibalism can be considered right to those societies that have practised it but wrong to those that don't, and whether issues such as this are relative to different societies and times or not.

This session can also raise interesting discussions around the ethics of meat eating, about which some children have already begun to think. It is very important, particularly with this session – though with all philosophy sessions – *not to reveal your own views on the topic*. If you do, then you are likely to hear what you've said echoed back to you by the children and you are less likely to hear the children's real views on the subject if you approve a certain viewpoint.

Cannibalism is an unpalatable subject at the best of times, and, for this reason, I suggest that you make a decision about its suitability for your class. If you decide that it is not suitable then simply leave out this story and make sure that you use the online maps that exclude this story.

Storykit
Names to learn in this story

- **Laestrygonian** (lie-stra-**go**-nian): Race of giant cannibals.
- **Antiphates** (an-**tif**-a-tees): King of the Laestrygonians.

Keyword list

- Six days and nights.
- Cliff harbour.
- Smoke.
- Odysseus plus 2.
- Road, well and big girl.
- To Antiphates the Laestrygonian.
- Wife.
- Antiphates and the spit.
- Horror!
- Argument.
- 2 escape plus chase.
- The harbour trap.
- One ship escapes.
- The last they saw of them ...

Storykit Hint: Adapting the story to suit your audience

One of the many virtues of storytelling is that your presentation is not limited to what is written. If a story has been written with a particular age group in mind, then it is very difficult to *read* to audiences of a different age, due to tone, humour or content. However, if you tell a story rather than read it, then it can be instantly adapted. You simply add or subtract longer words, adjust the jokes, or remove unnecessary characters and events for younger ones. You can also change the tense at will or the person-perspective as well as the tone and register (language used). When you have 'the telling' at your fingertips, suddenly all kinds of resources become open to all ages and audiences.

Synopsis for Dinner Guests (The Laestygonians)

They venture forth onto another unknown island and find a race of giant cannibals called Laestrygonians. Odysseus narrowly escapes being eaten for dinner but during their escape they are trapped in a harbour and the ship is pummelled with rocks. Once again they narrowly escape becoming someone's dinner.

Story

Again, imagine that you are one of the crew. For six days and nights the ship sails on until, on the seventh, you come to a new land, unknown to any of you. An excellent harbour is found in which to moor the ship, almost wholly encircled by huge cliffs that cast the ship in shadow and safely out of view. No signs of life or civilisation can be seen but for a wisp of smoke that rises up in the distance. Odysseus instructs two of you to accompany him to seek out the source of the smoke.

Having left the ship, the three of you discover a wagon road that is clearly in use so you follow the road to see where it will lead you. After some time, you come to a large well where you find a larger-than-usual girl drawing water from it. You ask her who she is and where she is from. She speaks very few words but you are able to ascertain that she is the daughter of Antiphates and that he is the ruler of their people, a people called Laestrygonians. *She points to a high tower further along the road and seems to indicate that her father lives there. She is not particularly welcoming but you decide to head towards the tower to try to meet with Antiphates.*

When you arrive at the tower you are first of all brought before Antiphates' wife – a very large woman indeed. The Laestrygonians, it appears, are a race of giants and this giant is a particularly well-fed one. She circles around you all, looking you up and down and licking her lips as she does so. You find her to be repulsive both in her appearance and in her manner.

'My husband will join us for dinner shortly,' she says, though she has not invited you to stay for dinner.

When Antiphates enters, you can see that he is also huge and he brings with him a retinue of soldiers and advisors. He sees the three of you standing before him and he says to his nearest advisors, though loud enough for you to hear, 'The game, it seems, has come to us for a change. There will be no need for hunting today.' He promptly takes out a decorous, royal napkin and begins to tie it round his neck licking his lips, as his wife had done. When the other Laestrygonians see him do this, they follow suit. Two of them have begun to light a fire over which a large spit, apparently meant for some giant-sized pigs, is being assembled. Antiphates finally addresses Odysseus, who has begun to look a little concerned.

'It is the custom of the Laestrygonians to honour our guests with the most revered form of respect. It is the custom of the Laestrygonians to ... mmm ... (how shall I put it?) ... to invite our guests into our most sacred of temples.' As he says these last words he grabs hold of his belly and shakes it so that it

Figure 12: My husband will join us for dinner shortly.

ripples. As he does this it becomes horribly clear what he had meant by his cryptic words. When he had said, 'our most sacred of temples', he wasn't talking about any building of brick and mortar. He was referring to the bellies of the Laestrygonians! The three of you suddenly realise the horror of your situation: they haven't invited you to stay for dinner, because you are *dinner!*

Odysseus takes what appears to be the only course of action open to you – he decides to try to reason *with the cannibalistic Laestrygonians: 'Illustrious Antiphates! Do you not see that it is wrong to eat another human being?'*

Antiphates smiles as he responds, 'All our lunches make the same plea, which is good because I do enjoy a good before-dinner argument. Okay, let's make a deal: if you can provide one good reason *why* we *should not* eat *you then I promise that we will not. However, if you can't provide one good reason why we shouldn't eat you, then you must climb up onto the spit like a good little dinner! So, I'm waiting ...' says Antiphates as he glares expectantly at you.*

Ethics of cannibalism/meat eating

> TQ: You are going to have to think quickly! Can you think of *one good reason* why the Laestrygonians should not eat you?

Nested Questions

- Is it okay to eat other animals?
- Is it okay for animals to eat humans?
- Is it okay for cannibals to eat other humans?
- Is it okay if they have done it for a long time?
- Would it be okay for an alien to eat humans if humans are its only way of surviving?
- Are society's values relative to the culture the values come from?
- Is everything relative?
- If there was a kind of animal that wanted to be eaten, would it make it okay to eat that kind of animal?

For the purposes of this PhiE, assume that the Laestrygonians are human (albeit *giant* humans). However, recall from 'Logos: Teaching Strategies for Developing Reasoning' (see page 13) that you could *if* (especially *either-or-the-if*) any suggestions from the class that the Laestrygonians are not human, then remember to *open it up*. For example: 'If they are not human then would it be okay for them to eat you?' / 'If they are human then would it be okay for them to eat you?'. Then, if they say 'yes' to the former but 'no' to the latter: 'Why is it okay if they are not human but not okay if they are human?'

There are a number of ways to conduct this session. Here are a few suggestions:

- Role-play: Have half the class play Antiphates and the other half play Odysseus using the split debate model (see page 20). They are assigned sides in the argument using this method.
- Debates: Use any of the other debate methods (see page 20). The 'walk across' method allows them to take their own position on the issue and so express their own view about the topic, though, of course, they are also free to change their mind.
- Present an argument: Here's an argument that was formulated by some 11-year-old children that on first glance seems quite convincing.

  Antiphates' argument:
  It's okay for animals to eat animals.
  Humans are animals.
  So, it's okay for humans to eat humans.

- During the PhiE session you could give the argument to Antiphates. Remind them that if they don't find anything wrong with the argument then Antiphates will eat them! (See *The If Machine*, page 124, and the online supplement, 'Aristotle and the Logical Syllogism', for The If Machine for more on formal arguments.) The task set by Antiphates, to find 'one good reason', is specifically designed to encourage the children to construct an argument of their own. Odysseus has simply said that it is wrong for the Laestrygonians to eat other humans; the job of the class is to try to think of reasons why.

- Alternatively, you could just run a regular PhiE session on the following Task Question: Is it wrong for humans to eat other humans?

In a PhiE session on this Task Question with some 10-year-olds, they began by agreeing that it is wrong for humans to eat humans, until one girl said, 'They need to survive, so maybe it's okay for them to eat humans.' I *iffed* the question to the whole class: '*If* they needed to eat humans (in other words, they would die if they didn't) *then* would it be okay?' To this, one boy answered, 'Yes, because they have to survive.' I used *either-or-the-if* (see page 73) with him: 'And if they didn't need to eat humans in order to survive, would it be okay then?' And he replied: 'It's still okay because it's what they like.' Many of the children baulked at this, but one girl offered an argument in his support: 'I agree because there might be someone whose favourite food is pig. If the pig could talk and said, "I don't want to be eaten!" he would still eat it.' The implied argument behind her point came out during the ensuing discussion: 'Just because we say we don't want the Laestrygonians to eat us doesn't mean that they shouldn't eat us.' [Presumably, on the grounds of consistency, given that we eat animals regardless of whether they might want to be eaten or not.] I should mention that one of the earlier arguments given as to why it is wrong was that Odysseus and his men *didn't want* to be eaten. I have included this little classroom insight to demonstrate the sort of discussions that can be had by children on this topic. But I have also included it to show that, given the chance, children can construct some very sophisticated arguments in support of some less obvious lines of thought.

Story continued ...

You are now completely surrounded by fat, hungry, strong Laestrygonians against whom it seems you don't stand a chance. Realising that reason is to be of little help here, Odysseus opts for plan B: to run away! He signals with his eyes and the three of you make a break for the door ... or window ... or whatever is nearest to each of you.

Now, because you are so much smaller than the Laestrygonians you are able to dart under their legs. Though they are bigger and stronger, you are much more nimble. *The three of you manage to escape from the room and run back towards the ship. The alarm has been sounded, however, and it is not long before you seem to have the entire Laestrygonian population on your heels. You are able to gain distance from them, as they are not very agile, but you are about to discover exactly what purpose the strange cliff-encircled harbour serves.*

As you scramble back onto the ships, you discover that you aren't out of danger yet. A host of strong, able-bodied Laestrygonians appear along the cliff top so that your ship is entirely encircled by angry, hungry, *Laestrygonians, all of whom begin to pelt the ship with large boulders. So many rocks are there, that your ship is in real danger of being sunk. Though the ship sustains a great deal of damage, you are able to negotiate your way out of the harbour-trap. Many of you are badly wounded but at least you are all alive ... and uncooked!*

Figure 13: You are now completely surrounded by fat, hungry, strong Laestrygonians against whom it seems you don't stand a chance.'

7 Choices (Circe and the Pig Men)

Philosophy

With this story we return to the theme of happiness and reprise the discussion from Chapter 2: The Lotus Eaters. By the time of Aristotle (4th century BCE), the Greeks had a word for happiness that is worth introducing because it is not straightforwardly a synonym but contains a very different concept of happiness that challenges our modern conception. The word is *eudaimonia* (pronounced: you-**die**-mon-ee-ya) and it literally means 'the state of having a good attendant spirit' and is translated variously as 'happiness', 'flourishing' or 'well-being', but it is significantly different from the modern meaning of 'happiness'. When *we* – that is modern people – say 'happiness', we often refer to a *feeling* or a *state of mind*, but for the Greeks happiness related not to a fleeting sensation but to an entire life: 'Call no man happy until he is dead,' said the playwright Aeschylus (though this has also been attributed to others), and he referred not to the pleasures of death but to how one's assessment of a person's happiness must be measured against his or her life as a whole.

Happiness for us is also a *subjective* feeling: what makes *me* happy may not make *you* happy so if I *think* I'm happy then I am, I can't be wrong about it. But *eudaimonia* is more comparable to 'being healthy'. I can be wrong about whether I am healthy or not, or about whether I am flourishing. So, *eudaimonia* does not have the same subjective status as modern happiness does. Also, for the Greeks *eudaimonia* is connected to the virtuous life: for the Greeks, you can't just be happy, you need also to be *virtuous* to attain *eudaimonia*. Socrates even went as far as to claim that a virtuous person would be happy on the rack ('the rack' being an instrument of torture)!

Storykit
Names to learn in this story

- **Eurylochus** (u-**ri**-la-cus): One of the principle members of Odysseus' crew. However, he has a subversive side that will play a crucial role in the downfall of the ship and crew.
- **Circe** (**sir**-sa): Goddess and daughter of the sun-god, Helios. Her island is called Aeaea (**a**-ee-uh).
- **Hermes** (**her**-mees): The messenger-god and helpful to Odysseus on two occasions during the *Odyssey*.

Keyword list

- Forested island.
- Odysseus explores alone.
- Smoke rising and stag.
- 2 groups and lots – Eurylochus to go.
- Eurylochus returns alone.
- His story.
- House and singing.
- Wolves and lions.
- Woman emerges.
- Eurylochus hides.
- Men eat.
- Transformation.
- Pigsty.
- Run away!
- Argument: to leave or not to leave?
- Odysseus leaves.
- Meets Hermes.
- Flower.
- Circe's house.
- Resists.
- Oath.
- The men's choice.
- Hospitality.
- One year later ... home!

Storykit Hint: Visualisation

Any storyteller will tell you the importance of visualisation as a key tool for storytelling: 'seeing' the events happening before you, as it were, renders the story much more than a list of memorised words. This is important for memorisation but also as a source for your descriptions and it helps you convey your own love and enthusiasm for the stories (see 'Enjoy the stories' on page 96). Taffy Thomas, the first Storyteller Laureate, says that you tell stories with two parts of yourself: the left side sees the image of the event in the story and the right side chooses the words to use to describe what you see, painting a picture with words.

It is significant that the bard in the *Odyssey*, Demodocus, is blind, for, though he is blind, he 'sees' what others cannot (it is *said* that Homer was blind too). Demodocus is described by King Alcinous as having been given a special gift by a god. For the Ancient Greeks, the Muses (or, more precisely, the one called *Aoide*, meaning 'song' or 'tune') were the goddesses who were more than just an inspiration, as *we* tend to think of the word – they were the *source* of the storytellers' art in that they gave the stories to the storytellers. They weren't just making it up. This helps to understand how the Greeks understood what we might call *inspiration* and it is worth noting that the *Odyssey* begins with these words: 'Tell me, Muse, the story of that resourceful man ...'

Visualisation and confidence building

There are many visualisation techniques for building confidence but I would like to share one that comes from the *Odyssey* itself, from the part when Odysseus arrives on Phaeacia, though I have not included this in my children's version. At the beginning of Book 8 (The Phaeacian Games), the goddess Athena, disguised as a herald, tells the captains and counsellors of the Phaeacians to gather so that they can listen to the stranger who has been wandering over the seas. She tells them that 'he looks like an immortal god'. Homer tells us that these words acted as 'inspiration and encouragement to all'. Athena then imbues Odysseus with a divine beauty and makes him seem taller and broader so that he will inspire the Phaeacian people 'not only with affection but with fear and respect'. One can read such passages in the *Odyssey* as a kind of 'cheat' for the hero – extra divine help that somehow undermines his own resourcefulness. This is sometimes known as the *deus ex machina*-effect (literally, 'god in the machine'), where gods step into the story to solve problems. However, it can also be understood psychologically, as a metaphor for his state of mind. And it is in this latter way that we can make use of the following visualisation:

Before entering the classroom, imagine yourself imbued with a special confidence, just like Odysseus after meeting Athena. Like Odysseus, you stand straighter, your shoulders broader, ready to bring 'inspiration and encouragement to all'. Imagine also that the Muse Aoide then 'gives' you the stories as fully-formed, visual-audio images in your head. Then all you need do is look to them and describe them as they happen.

Synopsis for Choices (Circe and the Pig Men)

The ship lands on a forested island. Odysseus spots rising smoke and lifts the crew's spirits by providing them with a wild stag. The next day, lots are drawn to decide which of two groups will investigate the smoke. The half of the crew led by Eurylochus go to investigate. They find a house and the men are invited to eat by a mysterious but beautiful woman, the goddess Circe. She turns the men into pigs – all but Eurylochus, who hides, suspecting a trap. Eurylochus returns to Odysseus and tells the tale but also recommends that they leave the island before it's too late. Odysseus decides not to leave the island out of duty to his men. He goes to Circe's house and, on his way, is met by the god Hermes who gives Odysseus a special flower that protects him from Circe's magic. He then goes to the house and eats but is not transformed. Circe surrenders to him and he makes her take a vow before accepting her help and hospitality. He insists that the men be returned to their original form. However, she is only able to partially grant this demand. The men have to make the choice – to turn from pig to man or not – for themselves. Most of the men choose to return to man-form, but some remain as pigs in order to remain happy. Odysseus and his men then accept her hospitality as atonement for her wickedness.

Story

Still sunk in grief from the loss of the other ships, the one remaining ship sailed on with nobody uttering a word until the ship came to a new land. It was a heavily forested island that promised safety and sanctuary from the sea and its perils if not from the men's own sadness.

Once ashore, Odysseus decided to explore this island by himself, taking with him his spear. He ascended a pinnacle and again saw a wisp of smoke rising in the distance and a chill ran down his spine as he was reminded of what had followed the last time he had seen smoke rising. He took himself back to the resting men to discuss with them the best course of action. On the way back he managed to spear a wild stag resplendent with a full set of antlers. Odysseus returned with the stag as a gift for the men and that night they feasted, forgetting, for a short time at least, their grief.

The next morning, Odysseus shared with the men what he had seen while on the pinnacle. The men, too, were disturbed by what this reminded them of and, consequently, none of them desired to investigate the smoke, so Odysseus came up with a plan. He split the company in two, one half of which was headed by Odysseus and the other by Eurylochus, a man among the crew who commanded authority. They drew lots to determine which group would go towards the smoke and which would remain with the ship. It turned out that Eurylochus' company would seek out the source of the smoke. This filled all 22 of them with fear, but they knew that they must leave. A short time later, they gathered their weapons and some water and set off in the direction of the smoke.

Odysseus' company began work repairing the ships from the damage taken in the walled-in harbour. They heard nothing of Eurylochus' company until late in the evening – at that time of the day when it is neither day or night.

'Odysseus!' said one of the men 'Look!'

When Odysseus looked to where his companion was pointing, he saw a man running towards them. 'It's Eurylochus!' said one of the other men, 'And he's alone!'

Eurylochus eventually reached them but he was breathless and scared. It took him a good few minutes to find the wherewithal to say anything.

'Odysseus, we must leave this island at once! Do you hear me? At once!' he said, between breaths. Odysseus replied calmly as he put his hand on Eurylochus' shoulder. 'Now, take a deep breath and tell us, from the beginning, what happened when you left to seek the source of the smoke. Did you find it?'

'I did, Odysseus, but I'm afraid it is another woeful tale,' warned Eurylochus. He went on with his story: 'We marched through the woods until we reached a house in a clearing. We could see the smoke we had seen rising from a chimney. Inside we could hear the most beautiful female singing voice drifting like a spell towards our ears. Outside, there was already a sign that sorcery was afoot: prowling about the garden were wolves and lions, but they were not like wolves and lions of the wild. They were harmless, running up to us and wanting nothing more than to be stroked and petted like domestic cats. Most unnatural! We should have left there and then! My men called to the voice before I could say anything, but I decided to stay back and hid behind a tree, suspecting a trap.

'A woman of great beauty stepped from within the house and she invited the men in. I could make out through the door that they were invited to sit at a table laden with delicious food from which she bid them to take their fill. There must have been some evil concoction in the food because, once they had begun to eat, something terrible began to happen before my very eyes. I saw the men's ears get bigger and their bodies fatter; their feasting noises changed into snorts and grunts, and a small, curly tail began to coil out from their bottoms. Odysseus, on my honour, they had turned into ... PIGS!

'The next thing this sorceress did was to take a stick and whip them into a pen where she locked them in and threw them food fit only for pigs: acorns and apples and the like. Then she said to them, though I knew not whether they understood as men or only as pigs: "For as long as you remain here – that is, for the rest of your natural lives – you will eat the best pig food there is. You will be the happiest pigs alive!"

'When she had gone back into the house I instructed my fear-frozen legs to run and I took my chance to get away. I ran and ran and didn't look back or stop running until I reached you.

'And that is my story, Odysseus. Now do you understand why it is with the utmost urgency that we leave this island?'

Odysseus stood up and took a deep breath himself and then said, 'Eurylochus! It is indeed a strange tale full of evil but I cannot leave this island.'

'What do you mean Odysseus? Of course we must leave this island or else we shall all be turned into pigs!' Eurylochus could hardly contain his indignation.

A mini-PhiE session

You may want to stop the session here to discuss what they think Odysseus should do. You could use the techniques described elsewhere in the book:

- Conduct a debate using any of the debate methods such as Walk Across, Formal Debate, Split Class discussion (see pages 20 and 21).
- Role play Odysseus and Eurylochus (in pairs, or groups).
- Or simply ask them the following TQ.

> TQ 1: 'What do you think they should do: stay of leave? Why?'

Nested Questions

- Are there any duties here that Odysseus should fulfil?
- Are there any conflicts of duties? (See below.)
- Are there any ways that the conflicts could be resolved?
- How can Odysseus make such a decision?

Duties and leadership

One class identified two conflicting duties: 1) Odysseus had a duty to fulfil his *promise* to the crew to get them home, and they saw this duty requiring him to try to retrieve his men. However, they also recognised 2) a duty of *kingship* that required him to stay alive and return home. This duty seemed to the children to require that he leave the island immediately. Framing this discussion, as they had, in the context of conflicting duties, I thought an excellent approach to this discussion. To bring the conflict out, you could require them, when answering the TQ above, to have to make a decision one way or the other. The justification for this is that Odysseus, being a captain, has to make a decision: he cannot simply say, as many of the children will, 'There are reasons for leaving and reasons for staying, so I'm not sure ...' This will give the children an insight into the responsibilities and difficulties of leadership.

Story continued ...

'I cannot leave this island,' continued Odysseus, 'because I cannot abandon my men. Too much calamity has befallen them already so if there is anything at all in my power that I can do then I must attempt to do it. I have no choice: I can do no other.'

Eurylochus looked at Odysseus in disbelief and said, 'Of course you have a choice,' but he could see in Odysseus' eyes that there would be no negotiation.

'Tell me, Eurylochus, the directions to the house for I must take that route first thing in the morning though it be the last journey I make.'

Extension Task Question

> TQ 2: Does Odysseus have a choice?

Nested Questions

- What is a choice? (Socratic Question)
- What is obligation?
- If you feel obligated then do you have a choice?
- Are you free to ignore a duty once you've recognised one?

Story continued ...

Eurylochus imparted the route to the sorceress' abode in a low, reluctant voice and Odysseus listened carefully.

When morning came, they saw that Odysseus had left before the first light.

Eurylochus and the others noticed that in his despair he had neglected to take with him his shield and spear. Maybe he had seen little use for them.

Odysseus walked listlessly through the forest. At length he stopped to rest in dark thoughts. As he sat on a fallen tree he saw a light coming through the trees towards him. He was able to make out the glimmering shape of a man surrounded by light. The man wore a thin beard and winged sandals.

'What brings you into this dark and forsaken place at such an inhuman hour?' asked the forest-walker, 'though, you do not need to tell me: I know of your plight and that of your men, Odysseus, son of Laertes.'

'I can tell you, however' continued the stranger, 'that you have arrived on the island of the goddess Circe, the island of Aeaea, and she has worked her mischief on your men. But do not entirely despair, for I can help you.'

This, Odysseus now recognised, was the god Hermes and he realised that he may yet stand a chance if he fought a god with a god.

Hermes handed Odysseus a white flower with a black root. 'If you keep this flower secreted on your person it will prove to be an antidote to the counterpart magic of Circe. She dissolves a potion of her devising into the food she offers her guests, but armed with this flower you will be immune to its effects.'

Odysseus thanked Hermes for giving him a chance to save his men and then, with the flower tucked into his tunic, he walked on towards Circe's house with a newly found resolve.

Finding his height again, Odysseus approached the house of Circe and heard the song that Eurylochus had spoken of. He saw the wolves and lions as they approached him like pussycats. He called out and almost instantly Circe emerged from the house and invited Odysseus to sup. He entered, sat down and started to eat. He looked at his hands to see if they would turn into hooves but they remained hands. Circe then whipped him and shouted, 'Off to the pigsty with you and join your friends!' But, just as Hermes had promised, no trans-formation took place. When her magic failed to work she fell to her knees and began to cry. She pleaded with him to spare her and implored him to tell her who he was and to explain why he was able to withstand her magic. He said, 'Before I tell you anything you must do two things for me.'

'Name them,' she said.

'You must first of all swear by the blessed gods to refrain from using your magic for mischief anymore. And secondly, you must return my men to their human form. If you do these things for me then I shall tell you who I am.'

'I shall do as you ask,' she said and then she swore an oath. But then she began to cry again.

'What is it?' asked Odysseus.

'I cannot return your men to humanity – at least, it is not an easy task.'

'Why not?'

'Because,' continued Circe, 'in order for your men to assume human form once more, they must decide for themselves whether they would prefer to remain as pigs, happy in their lot, or to resume their human situation, which, for them I fear is not a happy one. The important thing is that it has to be their own choice.'

'If that is the only way,' said Odysseus, 'then let us begin immediately.'

Circe stood over the first pig and uttered some incantation and a ghostly image of a man shimmered from the pig's back and hovered over the pig. It was the spirit of the man the pig once was. Circe addressed the spirit: 'Do you wish to return to your human situation, or do you wish to remain as a pig?'

The spirit replied with a question, 'Is it better to be an unhappy man or to be a happy pig? This is not an easy question to answer.'

'But answer it you must,' insisted Circe.

Happiness (reprise)

Ask the children to imagine that they are the pig-man.

> TQ 3: Is it better to be an unhappy man or a happy pig?

Figure 14: Is it better to be an unhappy man or to be a happy pig?

Nested Questions:

- Is it better to be happy or intelligent?
- Is happiness the most important thing in our lives?
- Can you name something more important than happiness?
- What is happiness?

This session is likely to have a good deal of overlap with the PhiE in Chapter 3, 'The Lotus Eaters'. You may simply want to continue the previous discussion. So, if for example you didn't manage to get on to 'Is happiness the most important thing in our lives?' or if you didn't manage to 'step out' of the story during that session, then you could move to a further stage in the discussion with this session. If you did manage to get this far then move onto the question, 'What is happiness?' and use the Break the Circle strategy (see page 15). When tackling the TQ above, be ready with some techniques such as the imaginary disagreer (see page 14) or one of the debate methods (see pages 20 and 21)

Story continued …

Circe addressed each and every one of the pigs in turn, asking each one the same question. After much deliberation, most of them chose to return to humanity though not one of them found it an easy decision to make. Some, however, chose to remain as pigs because they simply could not face the uncertainty of their human future. At least, as pigs, they would be promised happy, contented lives.

Once all this was done, Circe sincerely asked for Odysseus' forgiveness and in return for the wickedness she had shown them she offered to host the rest of the men on the island for as long as they wished.

Odysseus accepted her hospitality and the men were free to enjoy the fruits of the island. For a year they lived almost as contented pigs but the time came for them to think about moving on, for no amount of contentment could cure them of the longing to return home, not at least while they were human.

Extension Activity

Though this question should not be asked during this session, as it would ruin the plot for your listeners, it is a good question to return to at a later stage, or once the stories have been completed.

TQ 4: Seeing as all the crew die at sea, should they have remained as happy pigs when they had the chance?

Nested Questions

- Does the outcome mean that they made the wrong choice? (This question connects to the 'outcomes' discussion at the end of the Aeolus session.)
- Could it be the right choice to return to human form even though they die?
- If they could see into their future when Circe asked them to make the choice whether to remain pigs or return to human form, would that enable them to decide what to do? (This connects with The Underworld session.)

Under the World (Tiresias and the Underworld) 8

Philosophy

This is a popular session with the children – they find talking about the future and time very engaging – a challenge to those that say children don't enjoy – or can't do – abstract thinking. The question as to whether there can be such a thing as free will – if god, being omniscient, knows the future, and therefore also knows all our future choices and decisions – is a question that has perplexed the greatest minds in the history of philosophy and theology for millennia. I use the example of 'the stone' in this session, for the reason that it enables the children to talk about an undesirable future event without focusing on morbid or inappropriate examples like dying (an example the children often come up with). *Note*: if they do use a morbid example then simply tell them that you would like to use a less extreme example for the purposes of the discussion and then simply replace their example with 'the stone'.

Homer's *Odyssey* has a very interesting take on this 'theological biggie': when Tiresias makes his predictions he says that something will happen but he also leaves open room for choice. So, he predicts Odysseus' 'gentle death in old age' with certainty but, in the case of the cattle of Helios, he explains what will happen if they choose one course of action, and then, what alternative outcome will follow if they choose another course of action (notice how this ties in with the alternative endings given at Scylla and Charybdis on page 110). There remains some chance that they all return home, according to Tiresias. This creates an interesting parallel with the story itself and the act of storytelling. The storyteller, presumably, like the gods, knows the future events in Odysseus' life, so does that mean that Odysseus has no free will? Are *we* like Odysseus in the *Odyssey*? Could the gods (or the storyteller) be looking at our lives knowing exactly what's coming for us? And if so, does that mean that we have no free will? Further issues that are often discussed are: what is the future like? Is it already there for us to discover, or is it a blank slate waiting for us to determine it? Or is it, like Tiresias seems to suggest, something which is, to some extent, already written but which allows for different outcomes according to choices we make?

The Words of Tiresias

'The Words of Tiresias' is an original poem by the author intended to make the prophecies of Tiresias more cryptic and therefore more of a challenge for the class. It is also one of the devices used in this book to invite the audience to aid the story's progress. The poem should be photocopied or downloaded and projected so that every member of the class has a copy and it should only be given out when you reach the point in the story, 'The Underworld', where the words are spoken. You should resist explaining it all, and – where possible – offer the class the responsibility of interpreting it, which should include getting them to look up any unknown words in the dictionary. When you first read it, ask them to put their hands up at any point during the rest of the story, if they think that the poem may tell them something. Or, if this doesn't happen, then as you describe the salient features of a scenario, such as the cliffs of Scylla and Charybdis, remind the class of the poem and ask them if they think there is anything in the poem that may give a useful clue about the coming encounter. This affords a poetry/English/literacy aspect to the cross-curricula possibilities to be found within *The If Odyssey*.

Storykit
Names to learn in this story:

- **Tiresias** (ty-**ree**-see-us): Blind prophet who lives in the Underworld and who, unlike the other inhabitants of the Underworld, retains his mental faculties and his gift for prophesy.
- **Anticleia** (an-tee-**cla**-ya): Mother of Odysseus who died of a broken heart waiting for Odysseus to return.
- **Achilles** (a-**ki**-lees): One of the principal characters of the *Iliad*, the other book allegedly by Homer, that tells of the events of the war between the Greeks and the Trojans.
- **Hades** (**hay**-dees): The god/king of the Underworld. 'Hades' is also the name of the Underworld itself.
- **Persephone** (per-**sef**-o-nee): Queen of the Underworld.

Keyword list

- Circe: go to the Underworld!
- Tiresias the prophet.

- Set off – follow Circe's direction.
- North wind.
- River of Ocean.
- The grove of poplar trees.
- Where rivers meet.
- Offering:
  - Milk and honey.
  - Sweet wine and water.
  - Barley and prayers.
  - Ram's blood.
- A familiar face.
- Blind old man.
- Mother and a warning.
- Achilles' reply.
- Return to Circe.

Storykit Hint: The Bubble (making time for the story)

You can't do good storytelling whilst still trying to do other things. You'll lose the children if you stop halfway through to take the register or to send someone on an errand or to have a word with another teacher/ teaching assistant. The storytelling bubble is precisely that: a bubble. It's a special place cut off from the rest of the world but, like a bubble, it is also very fragile. The bubble is crucial for creating an atmosphere such as the one you will want for The Underworld story. Devote some time each week to your storytelling/philosophy sessions (usually an hour) and have a 'Do Not Disturb!' sign on the door during the allotted time. Minimise – to absolutely necessary – any interruptions to your sessions. (See also Storykit Hint: Tone and pace on page 116)

Synopsis for Under the World (Tiresias and the Underworld)

After they have stayed with Circe for a year, Odysseus tells her that they must leave. She is sad but advises them to travel to the Underworld to retrieve information about their future from the blind prophet Tiresias, who lives there. They follow her directions and arrive in the far north at the meeting place of the five rivers of the Underworld where they perform the necessary rituals to open the gates of Hades. Odysseus sees the familiar face of his mother but must first of all speak to Tiresias. When the old man arrives he tells Odysseus a cryptic version of his future that he will need to make sense of as he travels on. Odysseus also sees the dead spirit of Achilles, hero of the *Iliad*. Armed with the new information, the men return to Circe to restock before they set off on the next leg of their journey.

Story

Odysseus sat in consultation with Circe to ask for her help in returning his men home. She was sad to receive the news of his leaving and she had been dreading this day whilst knowing that, in time, it must come. She did not, however, wish Odysseus to read her secret thoughts in her face.

She agreed to help, as she had promised him her assistance a year earlier, and the first piece of advice she gave him was to leave in the opposite direction to home. She explained that he should first of all visit the prophet Tiresias who would be able to foresee Odysseus' future and offer valuable advice. But she went on to say that this would mean journeying into the Underworld, 'for it is within the dark halls of Hades and Persephone that Tiresias practises his art.

'He is unique among the inhabitants of the Land of the Dead,' she continued, 'in that he has been able to keep hold of his wisdom when everyone else there is but a flickering shadow of what they once were in life.'

'Though my heart is against it,' replied Odysseus after much thought, 'I shall follow your counsel and make my way underneath the world.'

The men were not pleased to hear about where the next part of their adventure would take them but they trusted Odysseus and so agreed to make the journey though their hearts too were against it. They stocked up for the journey and took extra sheep skins to protect them from the North Wind as none of them had ever travelled so far north to where the days are short and the wind is cold. They followed Circe's careful directions to allow the North Wind to carry them north across the River of Ocean until they came to the grove of tall poplar trees that marked their arrival near the gates of Hades. They then made their way, by land, to a rocky pinnacle where many rivers met.

Here it was, Circe had told them, that they must perform a ritual that would summon the dead. First, they dug a trench in the ground, then they poured their offerings into it, starting with milk and honey, then sweet wine and water; over this was sprinkled barley; then their prayers to the dead were made. The blood of a black ram was added to the mixture and with this the summons was complete. Circe had told them that they were to ward off, with their swords, all the apparitions of the dead that would try to reach the concoction, until it was that Tiresias arrived. Only he must be allowed to drink from the trench, she had said. Those that drank the mixture would be given the power to commune with the living.

Odysseus had no idea how difficult it would be to fight off the dead: not because they were strong but because of what it was he would see. Among the shadowy faces that encircled him in an attempt to taste the mixture in the trench, there was a woman's face that was familiar to Odysseus, and upon seeing her face, tears welled up in his eyes. Yet he was unable to let anyone else drink until he had spoken with Tiresias.

Eventually, the blind old man staggered forward out of the shadows, propping himself up with a stick. Odysseus allowed the old man to bend down low to imbibe the mixture. Upon swallowing a mouthful, Tiresias found a voice that echoed to the ears of the living. These were his words to Odysseus:

> *The gods see all and so see us,*
> *What has happened,*
> *What will happen*
> *And what just might;*
> *So heed the words of Tiresias*
> *To whom the gods have lent their sight:*
>
> *First, there will be the siren women*
> *But do not listen to their singing;*
> *Your freedom will come from not being free,*
> *From resisting to go where you long to be.*
>
> *The horror of the rocks you must not mention*
> *Don't let the crew know of your intention;*
> *If they know about the rocky death*
> *Then not one of you will keep your breath.*

Figure 15: For it is within the dark halls of Hades and Persephone that Tiresias practises his art.

Though you will lose six noble brethren
Better six than all your brave men
The choice is this, whatever you do:
The death of six, or of all of you!

You must resist the cattle of Helios
If you resist not then all hope is lost.
Hunger will come to everyone,
You all will die – all but one –
If you succeed in angering
The god of the sun.

You will return home, that much is true
But how you do so is up to you;
Will you return home all victorious?
Or dead? Or worse still, forgotten, inglorious?

Once he had finished these words, steadying himself on his stick, Tiresias returned to the engulfing darkness, back to the Land of the Dead. Odysseus would have to remember these words if they were to be any help at all.

Once Tiresias had vanished, Odysseus beckoned to the woman to drink the mixture. She came over and found her voice, 'Odysseus, my son,' she said, 'I am so relieved to see you in the Land of the Living.'

'Mother!' he implored through his tears, 'what calamity brought you into these unholy lands? When I saw you last, you were alive and well.'

'My son, like your father Laertes, your wife Penelope and your son Telemachus, I waited for your return but it became too much for my heart to yearn for you any longer. It was the pain of losing you – my beloved son – that brought me to my early grave. Odysseus: I died of a broken heart.'

This was a pain too much even for Odysseus' strong, brave heart. Three times he tried to take his dead mother in his arms and three times she slipped through his embrace as if she wasn't there. This wounded him much more deeply than any monster could ever do.

'But beware, my son!' his mother continued, 'take care when, and if, you return home. Your faithful wife, Penelope, had not married anyone when I departed but many suitors were pressing her to take a new husband, insisting that you were dead.'

The power of voice that the mixture had afforded her eventually faded and she fell silent. With her arms outstretched towards her son, she disappeared back into Hades, a shadow once more, leaving Odysseus anguished, his face soaked with tears.

Figure 16: This was a pain too much even for Odysseus' strong, brave heart.

After his mother had left him, Odysseus went on to speak with many other dead people before leaving that place. Among the many faces that he recognised he saw Achilles, the mighty Greek warrior who had played such an important role in the ten-year war with Troy until he was killed, struck by an arrow by Paris in the only place he was vulnerable: his heel. Odysseus noticed how he commanded the respect of the hosts of the dead just as he had the living. But Achilles replied unexpectedly to this: 'Odysseus, I would rather be a slave and live, than rule over every soul whilst dead!'

Eventually, they had to leave the gates of Hades and return to Circe's isle, having heard the words they had gone there for. The Land of the Dead is no place for the living, so they returned to the ship and set sail for warmer climes once more.

The future and foreknowledge

TQ 1: If you were somehow able to visit Tiresias, and he told you that tomorrow you will trip over a stone, then is there anything you could do to *not* trip over the stone? Or is there nothing you can do?

Nested Questions

- Can you change the future or is it something you can't change?
- Does the future exist before it happens?
- Do the future and the past exist?
- What is time like?
- Is the future predictable?
- Socratic Questions: What is time? What is the future?

> TQ 2: If the gods know Odysseus' future, does that mean that his future is already decided?

Nested Questions

- Can Odysseus have free will if his future is already known by Tiresias or the gods?
- What is free will?

Extension Activity

Tell a story, such as the beginning of Briar Rose (Sleeping Beauty), in which a prophecy is made by a character that has special access to future events. (Actually, Briar Rose has a *curse* but when 'telling' a story it is easy enough to tweak the original to suit your needs. As it happens, it is not important whether it is a curse or a prophesy for this activity, but it *would* matter if you were to run a PhiE around the story.) In the fairy tale, it is prophesied by a vengeful fairy that 'when the daughter of the king shall turn 15, she will prick her finger on a spindle and fall down dead'. Another, nicer fairy, softens the curse, though she cannot stop it, so that instead of dying, 'she will fall into a deep sleep that will last a hundred years'. Intent on preventing this outcome, the king has all the spindles in the kingdom destroyed. This raises the question from earlier: if you know your future, can you avoid what it is you know will happen? But this activity is *creative* rather than philosophical. Ask the children to *construct a story that makes the prophesied event come true even though everything is done to avoid it.* Can they come up with a creative way to *make it happen anyway*?

The Singing Women (The Sirens) 9

🖰 Philosophy

This story helps the children explore the philosophical topics of *freedom* and *desire* and the relationship between the two. It is usually easier to begin with the theme of freedom as this is more accessible to children and then you can approach the more complex issue of desire (or *wanting*) via a discussion of freedom. Conceptually, the key things here are to do with drawing distinctions. Is there more than one meaning of *freedom* and are there different kinds of *desire/wanting* in this story?

Homer's treatment of freedom is complex. It may seem that the Greek heroes are not free, merely pawns in the games played by the gods where the characters seem to be thrown about at the will – and the whims – of the gods. But there is more to it than that. Yes, the gods control a good deal of what happens to Odysseus, but he must still choose what to do in the situations he finds himself thrown into. This is similar to the notion of 'situated freedom', an idea of the 20th century French philosopher Simone De Beauvoir: that we are free to do what we choose but free only within the confines of the situation in which we find ourselves (social, economic, physical, etc. constraints) like an artist with limited materials available to her. This complex situation is related to the issues explored in Chapter 8: Tiresias and the Underworld during the discussion about whether the future is fixed by the gods, and is summed up in the words of Tiresias when he says:

'You *will* return home, that much is true
But how you do so is up to you'.

The Sirens provides us with a metaphor for a particularly sophisticated notion of freedom in a situation where it would appear that there is no room for freedom. Odysseus is tied to the mast, and so is not free in a physical sense;

he is also under the enchantment of the Sirens so he is not free in the mental sense. Yet he took a precaution, when in a rational and clear-headed state of mind, by tying himself to the mast and plugging his men's ears with wax, so that he would remain safe though he would lose his agency. This means that he has exercised his will from a time when his will is free to control himself at a time when his will would not be. As a parallel: if you are weak-willed around chocolate cake then do you think you have a free will to decline chocolate cake when someone offers it to you? If not, then do you think you have the capacity to avoid situations where you would be offered chocolate cake? If so, then this is the extent of your free will in situations where you have none – the extent of *your* freedom over *your* Sirens.

Storykit
Names to learn in this story

- **Sirens** (**sy**-runs): The sirens are in fact never physically described by Homer. However, later writers have described them as having the upper bodies of women and the lower bodies of giant birds as depicted by pictures on ancient vases. Their important feature is an ability to enchant with song. I have chosen to describe them, but only from a rumour.

Keyword list

- Odysseus leaves Circe – cheat fate.
- Wax and mast.
- Set off.
- Mist.
- Song.
- Rumour of Sirens.
- Under the spell.
- Last command.
- Escapee.
- Finally pass – Odysseus a broken man.
- First to hear and live!

Storykit Hint: Enjoy the stories (or 'rediscover' them)

The storyteller Hugh Lupton says 'only tell stories you like, stories that speak to you'. It is very difficult to tell a story successfully, no matter how well you know it, if you simply don't like it. This approach, however, would rule out loads of good stories, so here's my take on the matter. Sometimes a story just needs to be *reinvigorated*. You will draw pleasure from audiences that enjoy a story, so, if you don't enjoy the story the chances are the audience won't enjoy it and you, therefore, won't enjoy telling it. But if you tell it in such a way that the audience enjoys it then you will begin to enjoy telling it. See how it works? This is how you *rediscover* a story.

I have noticed that even the most hackneyed stories that I thought I didn't like have often found a new glow for me, when I've told them to children who have never heard them before. Suddenly I find myself thinking, 'Actually, I *do* like that story and I can see why it endures.' On this basis, I could tell the Cyclops story over and over again, even though it's the most well-known in the *Odyssey*. It is so well structured and full of excitement and ingenuity that children who have never heard it are enthralled and those who have heard it love hearing it again when it's told well.

Synopsis for The Singing Women (The Sirens)

Having returned to Circe, she is able to give more meaning to some of Tiresias' words. She tells them more about 'the siren women' (The Sirens) and 'the horror of the rocks' (Scylla and Charybdis). She offers Odysseus some advice not revealed in this story: not to tell the men about Scylla so as not to frighten them into the whirlpool created by Charybdis. He plans to pass the Sirens by plugging the men's ears with wax to stop them hearing the Sirens' song. However, Odysseus himself has his men lash him to the mast so that he can hear the music and live. One of the men has his wax come loose and he swims off never to be seen again. Eventually they pass by unharmed but for the pain Odysseus receives for having heard the music whilst being unable to follow it.

Story

When they returned to Circe's island they found that she too had some forewarnings of her own and she was able to give more meaning to the first of Tiresias' warnings. She told Odysseus all about the perils of the singing women for, as Circe said, 'only he who knows about them can guard against them. Foreknowledge is the sailor's only defence against the Sirens.' Tiresias had said:

'First, there will be the siren women
But do not listen to their singing;
Your freedom will come from not *being free,*
From resisting to go where you long to be.'

Regarding the second warning of Tiresias, 'the horror of the rocks', she offered Odysseus some advice that he knew would bring him pain when the time came to make the decision she told him he must make. The old man's words were:

'The horror of the rocks you must not mention
Don't let the crew know of your intention;
If they know about the rocky death
Then not one of you will keep your breath.'

Odysseus left Circe and returned to his men. He told them, 'It isn't right for only me to be privy to the prophecies of Tiresias and the advice of Circe so I shall impart to you what I know.' Odysseus told them all but one piece of information, holding – for now – to Circe's secret advice.

 ## Optional Extension Activity

There is a clue in the poem as to what the 'secret advice' is:

The horror of the rocks you *must not* mention
Don't let the crew know of your intention;
If they know about the rocky death
Then not one of you will keep your breath.

You may decide to give the class a chance to work it out at this point by asking, 'Is there a clue in the poem as to what Circe's advice might have been?' Don't spend too long on this however.

Story continued ...

With the information she had given him, Odysseus devised a plan to pass the island of the Sirens and survive. But being who he is, Odysseus did not simply think up a plan for their survival: he also wished to cheat fate itself. As Circe had told him, it was said that he who hears the music of the Sirens will surely die, so Odysseus could not resist trying to find a way to hear the music and live.

Upon his instruction, all the men filled their ears with wax so that they were unable to hear anything and then they tied Odysseus to the mast of the ship firmly so that he was unable to escape. Having done this, they moved into the open ocean once more. They sailed for most of the day and as the

Figure 17: Upon his instruction, all the men filled their ears with wax.

twilight of evening drew in, a sea mist rolled over the water towards them. It entirely surrounded the ship, making it very difficult to know where they were going.

Then Odysseus began to hear the music, as it drifted through the evening mist. He guessed they must be close to the island of the Sirens. What he could hear was simply the most beautiful sound he had ever heard.

What Circe had imparted to him in her account of Tiresias' words was that these strange and mysterious creatures lived on the island and, though no sailors had ever seen them and survived, it was rumoured that they had the bodies of giant eagles and the heads of beautiful women with mouths filled with razor sharp teeth. It was said that when ships passed by the island the Sirens sang their sweet, yet enchanted, music. Anyone on board who heard the music would be able to do no other than go towards it by whatever means possible, even if it meant jumping overboard and swimming there – even if it meant sure death! Just below the surface of the sea, surrounding the island, were treacherous rocks hidden like invisible spears poised to sink any ship. The Sirens then fed on the bodies of the washed-up sailors. Their bones littered the rocky shores of this terrible island.

Odysseus heard the music getting louder as they approached the island and it filled his heart with an unbearable longing to get closer to it. He shouted at his men to let him loose and implored with his eyes for them to untie him. But

Figure 18: Then Odysseus began to hear the music, as it drifted through the evening mist.

they remembered his last words before they plugged up their ears: 'Under no circumstances are you to listen to any of my orders except this one until we are well clear of the island. The order is this: you must not untie me from the mast! I will be the only way you will know when we are out of danger.'

When the music was at its strongest, one of the men, overcome with curiosity, pulled out the wax and his ears were filled with the music of the Sirens. The spell was so powerful that the man stood up and abandoned his oars; before anyone could stop him he had jumped overboard and was swimming towards the music, vanishing forever into the mist. He could do no other. Odysseus watched enviously as the man swam away to his death and tears of frustration started to stream down Odysseus's cheeks, soaking his beard. The men were deeply distressed to see their captain crying like a child but they continued to obey his last command and kept rowing. When they finally rowed clear of the mist and saw Odysseus slumped against the mast, defeated and broken, they thought that they must have moved out of danger. When they finally dared to unplug their ears and untied Odysseus he looked at them with wild, distant eyes and kept repeating, 'It was so beautiful, so beautiful and now I've lost it; now it's gone forever ...' The men took him below deck and let him sleep until the enchantment had left him and he was himself again. Odysseus was the only man ever to have heard the music of the Sirens and to have lived. Yet, from that day on, there would be an ache in his heart that would never leave him.

Freedom

When you have finished the story, explain (and write up) that there are three different kinds of person in the story. There is:

1 Odysseus, who is tied to the mast and has no wax in his ears.
2 The men who are not tied or chained up in any way but who do have wax in their ears.
3 The man who took the wax from his ears and who then swam away towards the source of the music.

Then ask the following Task Question:

> TQ 1: Which of these men do you think is the most free: Odysseus, the men with the wax, or the man without the wax? Why?

Nested Questions

- Socratic question: What is freedom?
- Can you have more or less freedom?
- Are you free if you are overcome with curiosity like the crew member who swam to his death?
- Are there different kinds of freedom? (See below.)

Some may say that it is the man without the wax who swam off because he was free to do exactly what he wanted to do. Others may object that he wasn't really free because he was under the Siren's spell. There may be those who notice that, though Odysseus is tied to the mast and therefore apparently not free, he is free to hear the music and then live his life, which no one has managed to do before. If you get a variety of responses such as the ones I've listed, then you may notice that the children are intimating, through their conversation, that there is more than one meaning of 'free' present in this discussion.

To help draw this out, use the teaching strategy *Carve it up* on page 16, and ask them if they think there is more than one meaning of 'free' in the discussion. In one class of 10-year-olds I worked with, they drew their own distinction between what they called 'physical freedom' and 'mental freedom'. When I asked them what they meant by these, one of them said: '*Physical freedom* is when you are free to *move* where you want and *mental freedom* is when you are free to *think* what you want'. Once they had made this distinction I then asked them to apply it to each of the three kinds of men and they said: 'Odysseus is neither physically nor mentally free because he is tied to the mast and he is under the spell of the Sirens.' They went on to say: 'The men with the wax in their ears are physically and mentally free because they aren't tied up and they are immune to the music. The man who swam off was physically free because he wasn't tied up but he wasn't mentally free because he was under the spell of the music.'

Positive and negative freedom

An important distinction in the philosophy of freedom to be aware of for this session is that of 'freedom from' and 'freedom to', also known as, respectively, 'negative freedom' and 'positive freedom'. The first of these, *freedom from*, refers to the freedom from external forces such as aggressors or the state. *Freedom to* refers to the autonomous freedom of the individual to act as they desire or will. Odysseus has achieved *freedom from* the Sirens and certain death, whereas he has no *freedom to* do as he wishes whilst he is tied to the mast. There are further questions as to what his autonomous will is whilst he is subject to the Siren's enchantment (see the section on smoking in the online supplement for this Chapter).

Advanced Extension Activity

In this story, when the crew member's wax is removed and he swims off towards the Sirens (and certain death), it says 'he could do no other'. Odysseus used the same expression during his argument with Eurylochus in the Circe story when he claimed that he had no choice but to try to save his men.

> TQ 2: Is it *in the same sense* that the two men 'could do no other', that is, have no choice?

The two senses are very different. In the case of the crew member, he is under compulsion from an enchantment but Odysseus is under a moral compulsion to try to save his men. The question is: in what way are these two compulsions different? The expression 'could do no other' comes from the famous line supposedly uttered by Martin Luther when he nailed the 95 theses to the church door in Wittenberg in 1517. He later said, in defence of his actions, 'Here I stand, I can do no other.'

The Horror of The Rocks (Scylla and Charybdis) 10

Philosophy

The word 'horror' in the title refers not only to the monster that lies hidden in the rock face, but also to the terrible choice that faces Odysseus when he stands before the rock faces. Choices and difficult decisions are not simply limited to adult experience. Children experience them too (e.g. 'Should I tell Miss that my best friend stole her pen or should I be loyal to my friend and not say anything?'). So, a session devoted to dilemmas is not only of interest to children but could also be helpful to them. In the story, I use the word 'anxiety' to describe Odysseus' state of mind and this has been chosen deliberately, if anachronistically, because of its association with the 20th century school of philosophy known as *existentialism*, in which dilemmas play a central role. I have also introduced to this story, what I call 'the politician's question' (also military leaders, etc.): *Should I choose A, where a certain number of people die, or B, where a certain number of different people die?*

Many people feel that politicians are wicked because they make decisions that result in deaths, but what is often under-appreciated, in some cases at least, is that there would be deaths whatever course of action were chosen. The politician is therefore, in a case such as this, condemned to making a choice that will result in deaths. Not easy and often not fully understood. This session may help the children understand the enormity – and sometimes the *inescapability* – of, at least *some*, politicians' decision-making. The scenario of Scylla and Charybdis serves as an example of what is known as 'The Trolley Problem' (see online for more on this).

Storykit
Names to learn in this story

- **Scylla** (**skee**-la): Monster with six heads on the end of six long necks that lives in a cave hidden from view.
- **Charybdis** (ka-**rib**-dis): Sea monster that lives under the sea and sucks in water, exposing the sea bed by opening the sea with a whirlpool.
- **Elpenor** (**ell**-pa-nor): A real character in the *Odyssey* but used differently in this version. Originally, he dies on Circe's island from falling off a roof whilst 'hung-over', unbeknown to the rest of the crew, only for them to discover his death when he is seen in the Underworld. It seemed apposite to give him his proper role, that is, to die, but to give him a more noble death.

Keyword list

- Odysseus dreads the only way.
- Describe what they see.
- Two cliffs.
- Whirlpool (Charybdis).
- What will happen if ...
- Odysseus' secret.
- Circe's advice.
- The Words of Tiresias.
- The choice: to tell or not to tell?

Alternative endings:

- A: The Twelve
  - Cheat fate.
  - Probability.
  - Lots.
  - Perimedes! Odysseus? No, Elpenor.
  - Six lost including Elpenor.
- B: The end justifies the means
  - Feeling and reason.
  - Six lost.
  - Odysseus' regret.

Storykit Hint: Eye contact, posture and breathing

By having the right body language you will convince your audience (and yourself) that you are in control. These hints are useful for both performance and confidence: by making eye contact, breathing calmly and standing well, you will make your audience feel comfortable, and consequently you will begin to feel comfortable too.

Eye contact should be maintained with your audience when telling a story. Try not to focus on just one person, however. Make sure your eyes address each part of the class on a fairly regular basis or some children will begin to disengage as they won't feel as though they are being spoken to. You shouldn't look like you are trying to remember something, as this naturally leads to a loss of eye contact as you look down to the ground or as your eyes roll to look up to the corner of your head. If you have to glance at your cue-sheet then, the moment you have seen your keyword, look up again. While you are looking at your cue-sheet you will lack confidence but the moment you look up to begin explaining what you are 'seeing in your head' then you'll find that your confidence returns. It is worth noting here that if you do need to look at your keyword list that you should not break the 'bubble' (see page 89) by apologising – stay in the story, glance at the word and then carry on (see also 'Memorising stories', page 47, for using pauses).

Posture tips:

- Shoulders down.
- Neck relaxed and in line with body, not thrusting forward.
- Chest out so that your body is 'open' in a 'giving' posture.
- Your feet should be flat on the ground, slightly apart.
- Your face should be towards your audience.
- Your hands should be free to gesture and gesticulate in a controlled way.
- Your body should be ready for movement.
- If sitting to 'tell', then keep a straight back.

Breathing should be relaxed, slow and rhythmic; your breaths should be deep and from the diaphragm. Shallow breathing often comes from being nervous and can result in loss of voice and other voice-related problems. So, be mindful to breathe properly for your storytelling.

Synopsis for The Horror of The Rocks (Scylla and Charybdis)

Soon after having escaped the Sirens they arrive at the narrow pass that houses two monsters, one on either side. On the left hides Scylla, the six-headed monster that feeds on the unsuspecting crew members of passing ships. On the right is a whirlpool created by the monster Charybdis that sucks the water into it. If they steer to the left, six men will be lost, but if they steer to the right, the entire ship will be lost. This presents a dilemma: the ship or just six men? However, there is a more difficult dilemma for Odysseus: should he follow Circe's advice not to tell the men of Scylla, therefore reducing the risk of losing the entire ship to Charybdis through the men's fear? They pass through but at some considerable cost; but what the cost is depends on the decision made.

Story

In this story I will ask you to take on two roles: that of Odysseus and that of the crew again. Listen carefully and you'll see what I mean.

You are greatly relieved to have passed the danger of the Sirens but little do you know what dangers lie ahead. What at this time you don't know is that Odysseus is dreading the next encounter even more than the last. If it is indeed possible for there to be something more dangerous than the Sirens!

Another day's sailing brings you to a narrow pass that lies between two cliff faces barely an arrow's flight apart. Forbidding as it looks, for you to be able to continue with your journey it is necessary that you pass through here – the only other way is through 'the clashing rocks'. But that way, you would surely meet your doom.

To the left of the pass is a cliff almost entirely hidden in dense foliage. To your right is another cliff with bare rocks, but at its base, under a single fig tree that hangs over it, is a terrible whirlpool that is sucking anything in that is within a certain distance of it. The whirlpool is the product of the mighty Charybdis, *a huge monster that lies at the seabed sucking in water to make this artificial mouth – the whirlpool – through which she is able to feed.*

It is clear to you from what you are able to survey that if you steer the ship too close to the right-hand side then the ship will certainly be dragged by the current and

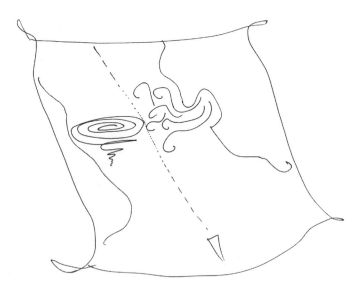

Figure 19: You will need to steer a true course between these two dangers to have any chance of passing through safely.

devoured by the whirlpool, but if you steer too close to the other cliff then you will be in danger of being dashed against the rocks. You will need to steer a true course between these two dangers to have any chance of passing through safely.

What you don't know – but Odysseus does – is that this is nothing compared to the real danger that remains hidden from you. Obscured behind the foliage in the left-hand cliff face is a cave. This cave is the entrance to the lair of Scylla – a ferocious, six-headed monster, each head at the end of a long, snaky neck. In her lair, Scylla lies in wait for passing ships whose crews are usually so preoccupied with trying to avoid the whirlpool that they are completely taken by surprise when her six heads shoot out to pluck six crew members from the ship's deck. The unsuspecting men are her prey.

Circe had given Odysseus some advice about 'the horror of the rocks', a phrase clearly meant to describe Scylla, and she had interpreted the advice from the cryptic words of Tiresias that Odysseus had recounted to her. The blind prophet had said:

'The horror of the rocks you must not *mention*
Don't let the crew know of your intention;
If they know about the rocky death
Then not one of you will keep your breath.'

[*PhiE*: If you haven't already done this, then ask them what they think Circe's advice was, from the evidence of the poem. See Optional Extension Activity in Chapter 9: The Sirens, page 98.]

Circe had understood this to mean that Odysseus must not tell the crew of Scylla because if the men know of Scylla then they will be too scared to get close to the left-hand cliff face. But in their nervousness of Scylla, a much worse fate will befall them: the ship will be dragged into the whirlpool where it will be utterly devoured by Charybdis. She reasoned to Odysseus that the best chance of survival they have is for the crew to be unaware, and therefore unafraid, of Scylla. The cost of this strategy, however, is that Scylla will be able to lay claim to six of the ship's crew members. Is it a cost worth paying? Tiresias also makes clear that there is no alternative third option:

'Though you will lose six noble brethren
Better six than all your brave men.
The choice is this, whatever you do:
The death of six, or of all of you!'

This is the choice, then, that Odysseus now finds himself with: should he tell the men of Scylla and risk their fear bringing the ship to ruin, or should he remain silent of the danger of Scylla, to lose six men in the process, but securing the safety of the ship and the rest of the crew? *The choice fills Odysseus with horror and anguish but decide he must.*

Dilemmas

The children should be invited to take the position of Odysseus when trying to answer the choice. This means that, as the captain, they are unable to shirk from the decision. Anchor them (see *Anchoring* on page 18) by reminding them that, as the captain of the ship, they must make a decision. Many children will prefer not to have to make it. *Note:* the children are very likely to try to find a third way in this session, but the whole point of a dilemma is that it is a choice between two positions that have been forced onto the decision-maker. In other words, *there is no third way.* You will need to *anchor* them to this stipulation. To make sense of this, use the device of Tiresias' predictions, who said:

'The choice is this, whatever you do:
The death of six, or of all of you!'

Figure 20: The choice fills Odysseus with horror and anguish but decide he must.

TQ 1: Should he tell the men of Scylla and risk their fear bringing the ship to ruin, or should he remain silent of the danger of Scylla, to lose six men in the process, but securing the safety of the ship and the rest of the crew?

Nested Questions

- How important is honesty here?
- Could the men be better off *not knowing*?
- Does Odysseus have a duty here? What is it?
- Is it better to lose six men or the entire ship?

If they decide, in the role of Odysseus, that he *should* tell the men of Scylla, then read the section below entitled *The Twelve*. If, however, they decide that Odysseus *should not* tell the men of Scylla then read *The End Justifies the Means*. You may want to get them to vote in order to arrive at a class decision.

At some point during this discussion, teach the children what a true dilemma is. A dilemma is a decision where neither of the options are desirable and where it is far from easy to decide which of the two options to choose. One way to get this across is to write up on the board the two options – A: to tell, or B: not to tell – with a weighing scale between the options, like this:

Figure 21: Odysseus's dilemma: to tell or not to tell.

Ask the children to distribute numbers between 0 and 10 for the two options, according to the importance the children give each option. For instance, someone may put 3 under A and 7 under B, whereas someone else may put 2 under B and 8 under A. However, the two numbers, when added up, must add up to 10. When, and if, someone puts 5 under both A *and* B, this is a good example of a true dilemma because it is not at all clear which of the two options is to be preferred. Even if someone has 6 under one and 4 under the other they have at least displayed a weighting in the direction of one of the horns of the dilemma, albeit a small one. This method of quantifying the dilemma is a method the children could use with other difficult decisions they have to make (such as, 'Should I stay at school at 16 or leave?', for instance).

Story continued …

Choice A: The Twelve

Odysseus decides that it would be more honourable to tell the men of Scylla and to plot a course of action together even if this puts the ship in greater danger. They decide that if they place six men on the left side of the ship in full fighting regalia then the men will stand a greater chance of survival against Scylla's six heads. But Perimedes points out that it was foretold by Tiresias that six men would die. To this, Odysseus devises a scheme to attempt to elude the certainty of fate once more.

'There is enough room at the side of the ship for twelve men to fight, is there not?' begins Odysseus. 'So, we should place not six but twelve men in their fighting positions on the left side of the ship. This is better because if six are placed to fight then the six will suffer knowing that their fate is sealed, but if twelve are ready then which six it will be that perish remains a mystery to each man. That way, each man's fate is not certain but only probable. We shall draw lots to decide which of us will be "The Twelve".'

Lots are drawn from a helmet. Among those chosen is Perimedes, Odysseus' companion, friend and the ship's navigator. The prospect of losing your only navigator incites one of you to shout to Odysseus, 'We need our navigator!'

'But I have been selected,' says Perimedes calmly. 'I accept my fate with equanimity and will not be bent from this course.'

'Then we may as well sail straight into the watery throat of Charybdis now,' replies the other crew member.

'I will take his place,' says Odysseus, seeing no other solution to this.

'No,' said Perimedes, 'they need you more than they do me.'

'What are we to do then?' asks Odysseus.

'I will take your place, Perimedes,' says a voice as yet unheard.

'Elpenor!' exclaims Odysseus. 'This is a most noble act, an act that can't be forced upon you. But if you choose to do this willingly then the ship and the surviving crew will be eternally grateful, but not as grateful as their families.'

'I do choose to take Perimedes' place,' says Elpenor.

'Then it pains me to have to accept your noble offer, noble Elpenor,' agrees Odysseus.

'The twelve', including Elpenor, assume their positions, armed with helmets, shields and spears, and the ship sails gently through the pass. A silence, as still and imposing as the cliff itself, sharpens your focus as the ship passes beneath the hidden lair, the silence broken only by the occasional creaking of the ship.

Then, almost without sound, the six heads dart from between the leaves and there is barely time for the twelve to move their spears. It is over in a matter of seconds as only six of the twelve are left to inhabit their bewilderment. The screams of the other men can be heard from behind the undergrowth, though nothing can be seen of their dismemberment as Scylla feeds upon their sacrificed bodies. The hideous sound of your comrades meeting their end is a sound that shall haunt your dreams for the rest of your days.

Once you are through the pass safely, the crew spend some time in sombre silence whilst you grieve over 'the brave six', that includes Elpenor, lost for the ship's salvation.

Choice B: The End Justifies the Means

Odysseus, in his horror and anguish, defers to Circe's judgement, so he resolves not to tell the men of Scylla. He feels no relief, however, having made this decision but he reasons that the outcome will be better for the rest of the ship if more people survive than die. If so, then the death of a few will be regrettable but a worthy loss. The reasoning rings true with Odysseus' head but he still has an unshakeable feeling in his heart that something is wrong with this decision.

You, the crew, steer as straight a course as possible around the whirlpool, getting as close as you can to the left-hand cliff and being careful not to crack the hull against the rocks that jut out from the water. Though you believe the greater danger to be on the right, Odysseus looks up at the cliff on the left with concerned eyes. Moments later you find out why.

The sound of rustling among the undergrowth draws your attention to the cliff that towers directly over you and you see only the snapping jaws of whatever it is that lies hidden in wait behind the trees. Before you have time to react, six of your crew have been snatched from the ship. All you see is the flailing arms and legs of the captured men, but though you can no longer see them when they are carried off behind the greenery, you can still hear the screams as they are torn apart limb by limb. You will learn only later what creature it was that was responsible for the deaths of your unfortunate companions.

Interlude: The Die and The Dead

In order to get the children to feel the consequences of their decision, explain that, because *they* are the crew, then 'the six' should be chosen from among them. Explain that who is taken by the monster shall be decided by chance.

Allocate a number for each child from 1 to the highest number of children in the class, probably around 30, by simply counting from one side of the circle to the other.

The Die: You need to find a way to randomly select six members of the class but you are unlikely to find a die with the right number of sides. You could ask the children to write their names or their numbers on a piece of paper and then select six pieces of paper randomly 'from a hat'. Alternatively, you could use random number generating software. There is software available for class computers and there are *apps* available for smart-phones. Using software means that you can randomly select from any number of children without taking too much time, as long as you have the software in place beforehand.

Although this should be fun and exciting for the children, it is worth bringing to their attention the gravity of the situation, by changing the tone of the occasion with the following ending to the session. You can also extend the PhiE by asking the children if the encounter with 'the die' has changed any of their minds about Odysseus' decision they were earlier asked to make.

Story continued …

Though Odysseus does not share this with you, he instantly regrets his decision not to have told you about Scylla. Regret strikes him hard immediately upon hearing the awful screams of the men he feels he has betrayed. Odysseus will hear those screams in many of his nightmares to come until his dying day.

Optional PhiE session

> TQ 2: Was he right to regret his decision?

Nested Questions

- Does the outcome determine the rightness of an action?
- Can an action be right whatever the outcome?

- Should he tell the men of his regret?
- Politicians often say that they 'regret' something rather than that they are 'sorry'. Is regret the same as being sorry?

Extension Activities

Dilemmas and choices (for Year 6 and up)
There is another dilemma here which resembles 'the trolley problem' (see online supplement for this Chapter). The dilemma is as follows.

> TQ 3: Is it better to lose six men or the entire ship?

For many (though not necessarily all), this will be a 'no-brainer' based on a straightforward quantity calculation. Therefore, to sharpen the difficulty here, introduce some of the following variations:

- If you could, or had to choose, which men should 'the six' be? The old? The weak? The voluntary? The leaders? A random selection? Who and why?
- What if you are selected to be one of 'the six'?

Probability
The strategy adopted by Odysseus is similar to the strategy available to certain species in nature. When flamingos, for instance, flock together in large numbers, the chances of any one flamingo being preyed upon reduce considerably. This is known as the 'safety-in-numbers' strategy. By doubling the numbers of the fighting men, their chances change from a 100 per cent chance to 50 percent chance of death. Find out about 'the Monty Hall problem' – a famous and very puzzling probability problem, the counter-intuitive conclusion of which can be demonstrated to the general puzzlement of your class.

Sacrifice

> TQ 4: Does the sacrifice of the few make sense if it helps the many?

Conflicts between 'the heart and the head'
Should you be rational when approaching a dilemma or should you instead trust your instincts and/or your feelings?

Contingency

In the story above there are two stories for different choices (*The Twelve*, giving an account of what happened if Odysseus decided to tell the men, and *The End Justifies The Means*, giving an account of what happened if Odysseus decided not to tell the men). Ask the children to write a story that contains a choice and then to write two different versions of the story giving an account of different outcomes of the choice. They should write one version of the story giving an account of what happens if the protagonist chooses A and then another version of the story giving an account of what happens if she chooses B.

Research question

Find out about The Clashing Rocks. What are they?

Clouded (The Cattle of Helios) 11

Philosophy

The Ancient Greek philosopher Socrates had a famous historical row with another group of philosophers called Sophists. The Sophists used to take money to teach people the art of *rhetoric* in order to be able to speak persuasively to audiences. In Ancient Greece there was a podium on which speakers would stand and address crowds of people in order to persuade them to elect them (citizens were mostly selected by lottery but some were elected). Socrates' problem with the Sophists was that they had no concern for 'truth' – they would show their clients how to be persuasive on an issue whether or not it had anything to do with truth. One of the most famous statements of relative values comes, via Plato, from a Sophist called Protagoras: 'Man is the measure of all things.' (See online supplement for this Chapter for a story about Socrates and Protagoras.) The name of this group of early philosophers has given the English language the words 'sophisticated' and 'sophistry'.

Clouds are a feature of this story in that the men become trapped on the island by clouds, Zeus gathers clouds to destroy the ship, and, metaphorically speaking, their judgement becomes 'clouded' by desperation and sophistry.

Storykit
Names to learn in this story

- **Thrinacia** (thrin-**a**-seeya): Island on which Helios' sacred cattle live.
- **Helios** (**he**-lee-os): Also known as Hyperion, the god of the sun.
- **Zeus** (ze-**oos**): King of the gods, also known as 'The Cloud Gatherer'. In this story you find out why!
- **Lampetia** (**lam**-pe-teeya): One of Helios' nymphs who acts as a messenger to Helios.

Keyword list

- Thrinacia in the fog.
- Helios and the words of Tiresias.
- Eurylochus' first speech: 'We are not like you!'
- Bad weather continues.
- 1 month later ...
- Prayers and sleep.
- Eurylochus' second speech: 'No dignity in starvation!'
- Odysseus wakes up.
- Too late.
- Helios' ransom.
- Clouds lift.
- The Cloud Gatherer.
- Everyone for himself.
- The Raft.
- The current of Charybdis.
- The fig tree.
- Lost again.

Storykit Hint: Tone and pace

On the whole, a calm, relaxed, rhythmically consistent tone in the mid to lower range of your voice is to be preferred when storytelling. And remember to pause at the end of thoughts, sentences or descriptions. This gives your audience time to create a picture in their imaginations of what you have said. It also helps to draw them in, ready 'for the next bit'.

In this story there is a good example of an extended action sequence, from the point where the ship is destroyed all the way to where Odysseus is cast adrift again before arriving at Kalypso's island. One thing after another happens here, so it is of paramount importance that you, as the storyteller, convey the excitement as it happens. Speaking clearly and knowing exactly what is going to happen is the first rule for achieving this, but you must also pay special attention to how you are speaking.

As the action starts to unfold, move out of your usual voice-tone and pace and gradually raise your tone as you pass through this sequence of events. Gather your pace, making sure that you climax at the point at which he looks to be swallowed up by the whirlpool. Give the audience the full impression that 'this really is the end' (pause) ... only to offer a lifeline for the story to continue at the last second.

This italicised section is perfectly suited for you to practise gradually raising your tone and gathering your pace and then bringing it down before picking up again. Try it to see what I mean, and then apply the same principles to similar passages in the story itself, such as when the crew make their escape from Polyphemus' cave to the point where they sail from the island but having lost one ship and some men in the process.

Synopsis for Clouded (The Cattle of Helios)

They arrive at the island of Thrinacia through the fog, and Eurylochus persuades Odysseus to allow them to stay there for a time. Odysseus is not happy but relents. He makes them promise to only eat what Circe gave them because he recognises this as the island of Helios from which he was warned by Tiresias not to feed on the cattle there. They do as he bids. But the weather remains bad and they are trapped on the island. They run out of food and become hungry. Odysseus goes inland to pray to the gods for help. He falls asleep and Eurylochus takes the opportunity to speak to the men once more. He delivers a powerful speech that persuades the men to eat of the cattle on the island but to promise to Helios to expiate for their transgression when they get home. Unfortunately, Helios doesn't see it like that and, when they eat the cows, the Sun god makes Zeus agree to punish them. The weather gets better and they leave the island but a cloud gathers over them and they are sunk by one of Zeus' lightning bolts. Odysseus is able to survive using his resourcefulness but he is drawn back to Charybdis by her current. He just manages to save himself by hanging on to the fig tree that grows over the whirlpool. She spews the water back up and he escapes. He is cast adrift once more.

Story

Soon after leaving the dangers of Scylla and Charybdis behind, the ship passed by the island of Thrinacia that belonged to the Sun god, Helios. This Odysseus guessed, despite the fog that had encircled them, because he could hear the lowing of the cattle that were so prized by the Sun god. He also remembered Tiresias' words:

'You must resist the cattle of Helios
If you resist not, then all hope is lost;
Hunger will come to everyone,
You all will die – all but one –
If you succeed in angering
The god of the sun.'

'We must sail by this inviting island,' Odysseus announced to the men.

'Odysseus!' replied Eurylochus in earshot of the entire crew, 'you are hard and tireless, but the rest of us are not as you. We are ordinary men and we are exhausted and grieving. Take pity on us and allow us to stay here awhile. And look to the sky: it does not promise good sailing weather. We would soon be lost again at sea if we dared to venture forth into this foggy ocean now.'

The crew applauded Eurylochus' speech. Odysseus, seeing that he was one against many, relented but made the crew promise not to touch even one of the cattle that roamed the island, but to take their sustenance from the food Circe had given them. This they promised to do.

As each morning arrived, they were greeted with yet more fog and drizzle, making it impossible for them to leave Thrinacia safely. And with each passing day, Odysseus grew more and more uneasy. His uneasiness came from his observation that they were running low on the food that Circe had given them. Just as Tiresias had said would happen, the men were becoming hungry.

A whole month passed and they finished the last of the ship's food. The weather was still unforgiving so Odysseus and his men were trapped on the island with hunger to test their resolve. In order to help, Odysseus travelled inland to pray to the gods for their assistance. Whilst there, and perhaps through the tiredness that hunger brings, he fell asleep. Meanwhile, Eurylochus was addressing the men with more of his honeyed words.

Class Activity in the Ancient Greek skills of rhetoric and oratory

Stop the session here and ask the children to compose Eurylochus' speech, either individually, in pairs or in groups. Use Eurylochus' first speech as a model (downloadable from the online supplement) and all they need to know is *that they will be trying to persuade the crew that they should kill and eat the cattle of Helios.* Each pair or group must also elect 'a speaker' who then delivers the speech; the rest of the class have to give a 'persuasion rating' (PR) where 0 = not at all persuasive (they definitely *will not* do what is being argued for) and 10 = very persuasive (they definitely *will do* what is being argued for). Collect everyone's PR and calculate the *mean (mathematical average)* by adding up all the numbers and then dividing the answer by how many numbers there are. (There is a cross curricula mathematics activity here: teaching what a mean is if they don't already know and then setting the task of calculating the *mean.*) This is done for each speech that is made. The 'Mean PR' that you are left with determines how persuasive their speeches are.

It is worth mentioning that some teachers who have seen the session have been concerned that the ratings given were not 'objective' and were too influenced by such things as who gave the speeches and what their friends voted for, and so on. However, unlike the necessary 'blind' vote in Chapter 5: Captain or Crew? (Aeolus and the Bag of Winds), where the aim is for the vote to be more objective, these less objective features are important aspects of a persuasive speech – people *do* decide based on the popularity of the speaker and how they see their peers responding. I would therefore suggest allowing these factors to remain so that they can be pursued as talking points about what reasons there might be for (and against) being persuaded by someone.

> TQ 1: If you were to get a PR of 10, and so manage to persuade someone of something, does that mean that what you are persuading them to do is the right thing to do?

Optional PhiE

Notice that this story provides yet another dilemma (though the class will decide during discussion whether this is a true dilemma) to do with the authority of the gods that the children can engage with in much the same way as with the previous story using 'the decision-making weighing scales'.

> TQ 2: Should they follow Helios' requirement and refrain from eating the cows, or should they disobey Helios and eat the cows?

Nested Questions
(NB: Some of these questions you will find more appropriate to secondary level.)

- Is it better to starve and obey the gods or to live and disobey the gods?
- Is it ever okay to disobey a god?
- If the gods decided that killing was good then would it be?
- If the gods decided that being helpful was bad then would it be?
- Is 'good' different from what the gods decide is good?

Extension Activity

Find something for the children to argue for (e.g. 'that they should be allowed to do what they want') and get them to compose a persuasive argument in support of it, but then, once they have done this, ask them to compose a persuasive argument in support of the opposite conclusion (i.e. 'that they shouldn't be allowed to do what they want'!).

Nested Questions

- Is it possible to persuade someone of opposite conclusions?
- Is it possible to persuade someone of something that you don't believe?
- Is it possible to persuade someone of something that is not true?
- Is it *right* to persuade someone of something that is not true?
- Could it ever be right to persuade someone of something that is not true?

Now continue with the story and give them Eurylochus' actual speech to the crew (available online).

Story continued …

'*Suffering brothers, listen!*' began Eurylochus. '*We are thin with hunger and there is little hope that we will reach a port that will feed us anytime soon and the weather may well stay like this for another month. If we do not feed from the cattle that are all around us then I fear we will die for certain. However, if we eat of Helios' meat then we are told that we shall also perish. So, I have come up with a plan to save us from what would seem to be certain death, whichever path we choose.*

'*To die of starvation is to die without dignity. It would be better to die quickly at sea by the designs of a god. But, maybe we can avoid dying at sea altogether! If, when we have killed and eaten the cattle here, we pray to Helios and promise that we will build a temple in his honour on our return home, and if we also promise to make a sacrifice to Helios every year from then on, we might yet appease him and he may allow us to reach home safely. If our offer fails to appease Helios, at least we will die at sea without the suffering starvation would bring, and at least we would die with our dignity.*'

Class Activity

Stop here and ask the children to give Eurylochus a PR number as if they were members of the crew. Calculate (or get *them* to calculate) the Mean PR (see above) to decide what *they* would have done if they were the crew. Then carry on with the story.

Optional Extension Activities

1) Use Eurylochus' speech for analysis and for teaching some of the techniques used in rhetoric, for example:

- He *identifies* with the men ('suffering brothers').
- He portrays the situation in the form of a *dichotomy*: a choice between only two options: ('A or B? both equal death!').
- He offers a way out ('A is bad but B is worse, so choose A').
- He strengthens the case with hope and attempts to remove the dilemma ('A has a *chance* of survival whereas B is certain death, therefore choose A!').
- He appeals to dignity and reduced suffering ('A preserves dignity and reduces suffering whereas B removes dignity and prolongs suffering, therefore choose A!').

2) Imagining that they are more critical members of the crew, set the class the task of composing *counter-arguments* (that is, arguments *against* a position) to Eurylochus' speech. For instance, is it truly a dichotomy (a choice between A or B)? Or is it what is known as a 'false dichotomy': a situation *presented* as a choice between A or B when in fact there are other possible choices that haven't been included in the presentation (A, B or C, etc.)? This could be either because the speaker has not thought of them or because the speaker is deliberately and dishonestly concealing the other options from his or her audience. If the class can think of a third or fourth option and can therefore show that it is a false dichotomy, then the question to ask them is *do they think Eurylochus was being honest or dishonest in presenting the case as he did?*

Story continued …

This was the second speech made by Eurylochus to find favour with the crew. And while Odysseus was asleep there was nobody to persuade them otherwise. They set to and killed the best cows of the herd, then they skinned the animals before roasting them over fires on makeshift spits.

Odysseus awoke, annoyed with himself for having slept, and returned to the men to find them resting after their feast. He saw with horror what they had done and he fell to his knees in despair.

Figure 22: They set to and killed the best cows of the herd.

'What have you done?' he said, as much to himself as to the men. 'You know that the orb of the sun sees all from its vantage point in the sky. Now we shall feel the full force of Helios' vengeance, of that I am sure.'

Here is the drama that unfolded in the halls of the gods following the slaughter of Helios' cattle – a drama of which the men were quite unaware.

When Helios found out about the offence against him from his nymph Lampetia, he straight away complained to Zeus, the king of the gods, and insisted on revenge to be taken by the Cloud Gatherer (Zeus' other name). When Zeus seemed unmotivated to do as Helios wished, the Sun god made a ransom demand: he said that if Zeus did nothing then he would take the Sun and shine it in the Underworld, depriving both gods and men of its light forever. Upon hearing this, Zeus agreed to avenge Helios.

The following day the clouds lifted from around Thrinacia and the weather changed so that it was suitable sailing weather. The men were pleased as this meant that they could leave the island of Helios and hastily make their way home. They also took it to mean that Helios had approved of their promise and was shining his light to help them home.

'Do not hope such things until we are safely at our own doors,' Odysseus had warned them. He did not share their optimism.

When they were alone in the open ocean once more, and no lands or ships were to be seen, a portentous cloud appeared over the ship and followed its course. No ordinary cloud would have done that. Shortly after, the cloud's black underside began to roll and a hurricane soon followed. The winds of the hurricane were so strong that the mast of the ship snapped off. Then, a lightning bolt flashed from under the cloud and struck the ship, momentarily lighting the sea around it.

The ship burned on the surface of the water and the men left alive were driven to leap into the sea. Bodies floated all around and Odysseus had to act to save himself; there was nothing he could do now to save his crew. Using a piece of leather he found floating next to him, he made his way to the broken mast and tied it to another piece of wood to make a very elementary raft. All he could do then was to cling to it and see what fate was to do with him. With the help of Zeus, Helios had made sure that the men would never reach their homes. For them, the journey was finally over, their futures no longer uncertain, their suffering at last come to an end.

The storm having abated, Odysseus became aware that his raft was locked in the route of some unknown current. The source of the current became apparent to him as he drew closer to it. The current was that of Charybdis as she sucked the water in.

There was nothing he could do to stop the inevitable, nothing he could hold on to or use to paddle with. The two rocks of Scylla and Charybdis slowly grew on the horizon as Odysseus drifted inexorably towards the whirlpool, his raft gaining speed as it closed the distance between them.

Figure 23: It was just a matter of time before he would lose his grip.

He could hear the sound of rushing water getting louder and louder as he finally came within the last stone's throw. Odysseus closed his eyes and looked forward to seeing his mother again: this time perhaps he would be able to hold her, *he thought to himself.*

Perhaps the last bit of his will-to-live left in him sparked in his breast and he suddenly remembered something: he opened his eyes to see the fig tree that hung over Charybdis from the cliff face. Without thinking, he threw himself towards it as the raft was swallowed by the spiralling water. Hanging from the fig tree, with nothing to get a foothold on, he looked below and was astonished to see the seabed at the bottom of the vortex. It was just a matter of time before he would lose his grip. Then it would all be over.

What Odysseus did not know was that Charybdis only swallowed water three times a day and she had just reached her fill. The whirlpool collapsed in on itself and a few moments later the water that had been consumed started to spew out again. It was just at that moment that Odysseus' hands lost their grip, but instead of being swallowed under the sea, he was propelled up into the air with a spray of water like that from a whale, and away from Charybdis. His raft also found its way out of the monster and Odysseus was very pleased to see it again. He boarded it and collapsed in sheer exhaustion, grief and despair.

The Concealer (The Island of Kalypso) 12

Philosophy

Love – like *want*, *freedom* and *happiness* – is a single word that hides many concepts. Deriving from the Sanskrit for 'desire', the word 'love' itself seems inadequate given the reach of this mysterious and complex notion. But perhaps one of the best places to turn to help us with the problems English leaves us with is Ancient Greek. The Greeks had many words for *love* and they really help us to begin 'carving up' the concept into further concepts such as 'the love of friendship', 'love of *doing things*', 'love of *family*', 'love for our *partner*', 'love for our *fellow human beings*' – and that's not to mention 'love for a *pet*', 'for *ourselves*', and perhaps 'for the *planet*' or 'nature'. See how many of these (or more!) the children come up with.

This session is also a 'maturity test' for your class. You will know exactly how mature they are the moment you mention the word 'love'. It is for this reason, however, that I think the session is really important for the class, as they show *themselves* that there is more to love than, say, 'loving football' or 'what my older brother does with his girlfriend'!

Storykit
Names to learn in this story

- **Ogygia** (O-**gi**-gia, g as in 'gig' not 'giant'): The island being the home of Kalypso.
- **Kalypso** (Ka-**lip**-so): Demi-goddess and daughter of Atlas; loves Odysseus.

Keyword list

- Nine days.
- Hallucinations.
- Carried to Kalypso.

- Whatever you want.
- 'The guest'.
- Beach-sitting.
- Watched.
- All the time in the world.
- Seven years later and an offer you wouldn't refuse.
- Poseidon goes away.
- Athena implores Zeus.
- Zeus sends Hermes.
- Hermes persuades Kalypso.
- The boat.
- Poseidon is furious.
- The Storm.
- Seaweed.

Storykit Hint: Clarity and enunciation

Clarity is essential when storytelling and it is a well-known adage that clarity of thought produces clarity of expression. So, make sure you know what it is you are going to say. Most of the time, knowing *generally* what's happening in the story will be enough for you to be clear, but there are times when more rehearsal is needed. Beginning and ending your story may need rehearsal, as the start is when you are most likely to be nervous, and because the end is the bit that your audience will leave the session with, it needs to be clear, leaving them wanting more.

There are other parts that may also need special attention. For instance, when Kalypso offers Odysseus his (false) choice, *'You may leave this island only when you have either learned to love me...'*, umming and ahhing around such central lines will take the edge off your storytelling, so make sure you know what it is you are going to say. Clarity doesn't come only from what you think but also from how you speak. Accents shouldn't matter but enunciation does. Try not to mumble your lines. Here are a few optional exercises that should help to prepare for storytelling, or, for that matter, any public speaking situation you find yourself in:

1 Open your mouth reasonably wide and roll your tongue around the circle of your lips, first from left to right and then from right to left.
2 Tighten your lips to make an 'ooooh' sound and then smile widely to make an 'eeeeee' sound. Repeat this action, getting gradually quicker.
3 Say the following sound-sentence repeatedly and quickly (with a short, closed vowel sound for the b, d and g, opening the vowel for the bah): 'b-d-g-bah'. Try changing the vowel sound at the end of each one: 'b-d-g-bah, b-d-g-bee, b-d-g-bor, b-d-g-boh ..', and so on. *Note*: Any tongue-twister sentence makes for a good warm-up exercise.

4 Touch your nose with your tongue and then try to touch the bottom of your chin with your tongue.

Synopsis for The Concealer (The Island of Kalypso)

After nine days of drifting at sea, Odysseus eventually arrives at the island of Ogygia, the home of Kalypso. Unconscious, he is brought to her and she nurses him back to health and promptly falls in love with him. When he awakes she explains that he is her 'guest' but it quickly becomes apparent that he is really her prisoner. She demands that he love her and become her husband. He refuses and longs to return home. Kalypso tries to tempt him by providing him with his every want and need and even offering him immortality, but Odysseus still refuses. He is 'a guest' of hers for a total of seven years. His escape, however, is secured by Athena, while Poseidon is away. Hermes is sent to inform Kalypso that she must release Odysseus. She builds him a boat and he eventually leaves. Poseidon returns and is furious to find Odysseus free, so he releases a storm that sinks his boat and nearly drowns him. He is saved by some sea-nymphs sent by Athena and brought safely to the shores of the Phaeacians.

Story

For nine long days he drifted aimlessly through the ocean with no shelter from the rain and the sun and with no fresh water or food to eat and drink. He had managed to catch a seabird at one point and when it rained he lay on his back with his mouth open to catch a drink. This served to keep him alive, but barely. As each day passed he became more and more delirious. The days blurred and he began to see all kinds of apparitions that were born of his water-starved brain.

His hallucinations seemed to be at their worst when, on the tenth day, his raft made the sound of hitting a beach. Looking over the side he found that he had arrived on an island but when he had surveyed the horizon just a minute earlier he was sure that he had seen no sign of land, just an endless expanse of water, glistening in the sunlight.

Hallucination or not, Odysseus had reached the point where he could go no further. He stepped from the raft onto whatever substance would hold him up, or into the sea. Strangely, his foot found under it a sandy ground, and he then fell down onto the beach quite unconscious.

It was no hallucination, but it was true that he had seen no island before his raft had touched it. This was because the island to which his little boat had drifted was hidden by a strange power. Only when a boat or foot touches this island will it reveal itself and only then to he who rests upon it. The island is the island of Ogygia, and the power that conceals it, that of the Sea-Nymph Kalypso, whose name means 'Concealer'.

While Odysseus' helpless body lay on the beach, two women advanced to his side and carried him to a cave where he was brought before another woman. The woman to whom he had been brought was Kalypso herself. When her eyes fell upon the face of Odysseus, though it was rough and emaciated and heavily bearded, love entered her heart. For several days she gazed upon this mortal man while he slept deeply, his troubles temporarily forgotten. Her maids tended to him and some days later he awoke, bewildered and hungry. Food and water were brought to him and Odysseus fed himself back to life, though with waking, he was reminded of his sorry situation.

'I am Kalypso, ruler of this island,' the Nymph told Odysseus, 'and you are most welcome as my guest here on Ogygia. Whatever you desire or need, I, or one of my servants, shall provide. I wish you to be happy here and to want for nothing and I hope that you will remain here as my guest.'

'I am deeply honoured and grateful to you for your offer of hospitality,' replied Odysseus, 'but when I am well I plan to return to my home, to my wife and son, who is now a grown man.'

'Your wife?' queried Kalypso.

Figure 24: The Sea-Nymph Kalypso, whose name means 'Concealer'.

'Yes,' said Odysseus, 'for I have not seen her now for many years and I yearn to hold her again in my arms before it is too late.'

'I am afraid that is one desire I cannot quench,' said Kalypso in a lowered tone. 'Yet you may love me *instead*. Kalypso *will make you happy*, Kalypso *will heal your longing* and Kalypso *will offer a new home for you if you would just become her husband*.' She looked at Odysseus trying to read his thoughts but she could not.

At long last she said, with a serious tone, 'Then here is your choice, Odysseus: you shall either learn to love me, or remain on this island as 'my guest' for the rest of your days. Think on it and give me your decision soon.'

Love

As quite a few children have pointed out for themselves, you will notice that 'Kalypso's choice' is a 'false choice' because if Odysseus does learn to love her then, because he loves her, he won't want to leave, and presumably Kalypso knows this; if, on the other hand, he doesn't learn to love her then he has to stay on the island. So, it seems that her 'choice' leads only to his staying on the island despite her saying that the first horn of the choice is the condition for his leaving. It is what is known as a catch-22. His only way off the island, it would seem, is to *appear* to have learnt to love her. But can he really do this?

> TQ: What should Odysseus do? Should he learn to love Kalypso or remain imprisoned on the island forever?

Nested Questions

- Is it possible to *learn* to love someone?
- Can you choose who you love?
- Does Odysseus have the right to disobey a goddess?
- Is Kalypso's choice to Odysseus a genuine choice? Does Odysseus really have a choice?
- Socratic Question: What is love?
- Are there different kinds of love? How many, and what different kinds are there?
- Can you fake loving someone?
- If Kalypso, being a goddess, can read his mind then could he fool her into thinking that he loves her?
- How do you know what someone else is thinking or feeling?
- How do you know if someone loves you?

You will probably begin to notice during a discussion of what love is that the children start to, either implicitly or explicitly, draw distinctions around the concept of love. Try to make, as a feature of this session, a version of *Break the circle* (see page 15) or *Carve it up* (see page 16) activities on 'love', so that the children identify as many different kinds of love as possible. Once they have done this, then introduce them to some of the many Ancient Greek words for love, contrasted with our single word in English. Match them up with the different conceptions that the children have identified. (If you have begun doing the course in Ancient Greek with the children, then write these words in Greek first and, as an Extension Activity, ask them to transliterate them before introducing their meanings.)

- Eros (pronounced **e**-ross, and written in Ancient Greek: ερος) = 'romantic love', the sort had between romantic partners.
- Philia (**fi**-leeya, Greek: φιλια) = 'friendship love', the sort had between friends. And ...
- Philia = 'love of activities', like when you love football or singing (or philosophy!).
- Agape (**a**-ga-pay, Greek: αγαπη) = 'love of all humankind', the sort talked about in the Bible when it says to 'love thy neighbour').
- Storge (**stor**-gay, Greek: στοργη) = 'family-love', the sort had by mother and son, father and daughter, or child and grandparent.

- *Follow-up question*: Have you, or can you, come up with more kinds of love than this? What are they?
- *Research question*: Does Ancient Greek have more words for love than these?

As an aside, it is worth relating that during this part of the session, one class of 10-year-olds I was working with suggested a solution to 'Kalypso's choice': they said that he could learn to love her in the *philia* sense of the word 'love' – an elegant and ingenious solution. However, there is a problem with this that another class of the same age pointed out: they said that because Kalypso is Greek she would speak Ancient Greek so when she said her 'choice' – *that Odysseus must learn to love her or stay on the island for the rest of his life* – she would have said 'eros' when she said 'learn to love me'. A very sophisticated dialogue had between two classes!

The final part of the session is to ask them to identify the different kinds of love had between different characters in the story.

What kind of love is (or was) had between the following characters in the story? (Are there any new kinds of love here?)

1 Kalypso and Odysseus?
2 Odysseus and Kalypso?
3 Odysseus and Penelope (his wife)?
4 Odysseus and Anticleia (his mother)?
5 Odysseus and Telemachus (his son)?
6 Odysseus and Perimedes (his close friend and shipmate)?
7 Odysseus and his crew?
8 Odysseus and the Ithacans (his subjects)?
9 Odysseus and all the other Greeks?
10 Odysseus and Argus (his faithful hunting dog of old)?
11 Odysseus and Zeus (the king of the gods)?

One girl said that the love between Odysseus and Penelope was all of the Greek words: *eros, philia, storge* and *agape*!

Story continued …

So, Odysseus had found himself trapped on Ogygia through a design he would never have been able to predict. Never would he have thought that he would be held prisoner by someone who claimed to love him.

Though he could have anything he wanted on this beautiful island, each day he would take himself down to the beach and he would sit and stare out to sea hour after hour with an ache in his heart. And hidden behind the trees, Kalypso would, in her turn, watch him, wondering where his thoughts were taking him. All she could guess was that it was away from her.

With each day that passed, his yearning for home grew stronger and with each passing day Kalypso's determination to wait also grew. 'He will learn to love me. I can wait,' she said to herself each day.

A year passed in this way, then two, then three years. After three years had passed, suspecting that Odysseus was playing 'hard-to-get', Kalypso offered him the gift of immortality in return for his love and tried to tempt him with her undying beauty. She reminded him that his wife, Penelope, would be growing old whilst he remained Kalypso's guest. Four years passed and Odysseus still had not given his love to Kalypso, preferring to grow old with Penelope – if he were to ever leave this place – than to remain with someone, however beautiful, whom he did not love. Five years passed, then six and seven. Kalypso was still waiting for him to love her and she would have waited

Figure 25: He would stare out to sea hour after hour with an ache in his heart.

until he left this world. An intervention of the gods would eventually decide his fate.

Poseidon was very pleased to see what had befallen Odysseus and each day he would look on at Odysseus' situation with gladness. Polyphemus, it seemed, had achieved his revenge.

One day, when Poseidon was away receiving sacrifices at the far reaches of the world in Ethiopia, Athena, who had been keeping an eye on Odysseus and who had pitied him in his incarceration, stole the opportunity to effect his release while Poseidon was absent. She went to see Zeus, imploring him to allow Odysseus' release, suggesting that Odysseus had been punished enough. Zeus eventually agreed and sent Hermes to persuade Kalypso to release him.

Hermes had to employ a great deal of persuasion, as a love-struck heart is not one that is open to reason. But eventually Kalypso relented and said that she would let Odysseus go – perhaps her greatest act of love towards Odysseus. Hermes told her that she was not solely to grant him permission to go but must also provide the means with which to leave Ogygia. Reluctantly, she relented to this further request too.

A boat was built and with it so, too, was Odysseus' spirit. Though it pleased Kalypso to see him finally happy, at the same time it pained her to see him readying himself to leave with no visible concern for their parting. Yet she honoured her agreement to Hermes.

Odysseus said his farewell to Kalypso and told her that he had learned to love her in some way. He thanked her for her unending hospitality and he left her, sailing out into the ocean once more. After seven years ashore he was happy to be at sea again. But, strangely, you may think, he did not resent Kalypso for keeping him hidden from the world for seven years; if anything, he pitied her.

But the final leg of the journey was not fated to be easy for Odysseus. When Poseidon eventually returned home from Ethiopia he was furious that Odysseus had been released in his absence. The Earthshaker (Poseidon's other name) took his trident and whipped up another terrible storm to seek out Odysseus. His little boat was no match for Poseidon's wrath and it was soon dashed against the waves as though they were rocks. Odysseus found himself floating in the sea unable to swim up to put his head above the surface, the currents of Poseidon's storm dragging him down and down. His breath was eventually spent and the last thing he was aware of before he passed out was the gentle touch of what he took to be seaweed against his ankles as the depths claimed him.

The touch was not, however, that of seaweed but the delicate, life-saving fingers of sea nymphs sent by Athena. The nymphs guided him back to the surface and allowed him to take in the sweet air above. Then they guided him to the shores of yet another island and left him to find his senses again under the cool, bracing air of the morning.

Extension Activity

Optional literacy extension activity

How many different examples of – or references to – *concealment* can the children identify in this story?

13 The Storyteller (The Phaeacians)

Philosophy

Children have a habit of identifying themselves with their name. The question 'Who would you be without a name?' on some occasions, with very young children, has elicited the answer: 'Nobody.' In his book *Love, Sex and Tragedy: How the Ancient World Shapes Our Lives*, Simon Goldhill points out the dangers of identifying ourselves only with our name. He tells the story of Pentheus, from Eurypides' play *The Bacchae*, who answers the question put to him by the god Dionysus, 'Who are you?', with his name, his family and his position. Dionysus replies, 'You do not know what your life is, nor what you are doing, nor who you are?'

Following a story about a boy with no name and in answer to the question 'Who would you be without a name?', one six-year-old girl said, 'Even if you don't have a name, you are still *somebody* because you still *think* and *like things*, and you're still *there*.' She clearly shared Dionysus' concerns over the insufficiency of identifying yourself with your name. A boy in the same class said, 'He's not *nobody*, he's *somebody*.' When asked why, he said, 'Because he's still *in* the story.'

The children had identified several important aspects of identity that go beyond one's name, family and position. These are: a) thinking; b) wants and desires ('... you still *think* and *like things* ...' said the girl); and c) the stuff you are made of, or what philosophers call your *numerical* identity ('... you're still *there* ...' said the boy). But when the boy said, 'he's still *in* the story', he had unwittingly alluded to one of the lesser-known theories of identity: *narrative* identity, as discussed by the philosopher Alistair MacIntyre in his book *After Virtue*. The idea behind narrative identity is that the classic criteria for personal identity – memory and body – are insufficient for our identity because we still have to make sense of how our memories and our bodies fit into a narrative structure. In other words, we need to understand ourselves within the context of a story – the story of our lives – and that story, in turn, needs to be understood in the context of the story of others' lives also.

This Chapter addresses two criteria for personal identity: *memory* and *narrative identity*. In this version of the *Odyssey*, Odysseus loses his memory – a 'tweak' of my own. This allows the perennial philosophical favourite of *identity through memory* into the PhiE aspect of the chapter. When Odysseus is asked by Alcinous, 'Who are you?', his first answer is, as with Pentheus: 'I am Odysseus, son of Laertes.' Then he identifies himself with the Odysseus of the wooden horse story that they have just heard from the lips of Demodocus. Yet this only makes sense to his audience when he goes on to *tell* his story: the story of the *Odyssey*, no less – or at least, part of it. Assuming that Odysseus is fictional, then the narrative-criteria is essential for his identity in that he is *nothing other* than his story. But what a story!

Storykit
Names to learn in this story

- **The Phaeacians** (Fay-**ee**-shuns): Inhabitants of the island of Phaeacia, favoured by the gods.
- **Nausicaa** (**Nor**-si-ka): Daughter of King Alcinous. Older and infatuated with Odysseus in Homer's version, but I have made her parallel the age of most of my listeners, somewhere between 10 and 14 years of age. I have reconceived the scenes with her to act as light relief for my audience.
- **Alcinous** (**Al**-si-nus): King of the Phaeacians. A good and helpful man.
- **Leetho** (**Lee**-thow): Odysseus' alter ego in this story. It is the name given him by Nausicaa after she finds him with no memory. In Ancient Greek this word means 'forget'. One of the five rivers of the Underworld is called *Lethe*, and it has the power to erase the memories of anyone who drinks from it.
- **Laodamus** (Lay-**oh**-da-mus): The son of Alcinous and one of the competing athletes at the Phaeacian games.
- **Demodocus** (De-**mo**-di-cus): The blind bard, thought to be based on Homer himself, also said to be blind. He is our (i.e. the storytellers') secret hero!
- **Halitherses** (Ha-li-**ther**-sis): A seer who warned Odysseus that if he left for the war against Troy he would not return for 20 years.

Keyword list

- Another beach and lost memory.
- The girl (Nausicaa).
- Leetho.
- To her father.

- Does as he's told!
- The games.
- Food and entertainment.
- Demodocus the storyteller.
- Odysseus the madman.
- The Wooden Horse.
- Odysseus cries.
- He remembers.
- Odysseus the storyteller.
- Help at last.
- Home.
- The mysterious woman.

Storykit Hint: Adopting multiple storytelling points of view

The storyteller is not just a narrator. Of course, sometimes the teller *is* the narrator ('the ship sailed for many days on the ocean before land was spotted ...'), but at other times the teller is the speaker of dialogue ('I most certainly *will not*. What kind of a dragon do you take me for?'). When speaking, the teller *becomes* the character, often adopting appropriate voices and facial expressions on behalf of the speaking character. If the teller describes something like an eagle flying over, for instance, they can inhabit different points-of-view for the audience: the teller can spread out her arms as she explains that the eagle is flying over. In this case, the teller has *inhabited* the eagle itself. However, she may 'look up' as she speaks, inhabiting one of the characters that 'sees' the eagle from the road below. Her actions can inhabit different characters' points-of-view from sentence to sentence. Leaping from body to body, the teller hops effortlessly from character-to-character, even object-to-object, point-of-view to point-of-view. This is just one of the many ways the storyteller can bring the story to life.

A story within a story

This Chapter gives the storyteller the opportunity to really make use of this particular virtue of the storytelling art. When the character of Demodocus tells the story of Odysseus the madman – a *story within a story* – it is important to distinguish Demodocus' voice from that of the narrator so that the listeners know that it's a story within a story. Done well, it should be easy for your audience to follow; done badly, it is likely to lead only to confusion. To achieve this effect effortlessly you can pull on a variety of techniques: you could:

- adopt a distinctive voice or accent for Demodocus;
- physicalise him with your hands and body;

- make use of props and throw a cloak over your back and hold a stick in front of you;
- insert the words 'said Demodocus' reasonably frequently into the story.

Alternatively, you could try all – or a combination – of the options together.

Synopsis for The Storyteller (The Phaeacians)

Odysseus wakes to find himself on the beach of the Phaeacians but he doesn't know where he is, and, what's more, he has lost his memory. He is found by Nausicaa, the daughter of King Alcinous. As he can't remember his name, she gives him one – Leetho – and takes him to her father insisting that Alcinous take care of him. Odysseus – known to everyone there as Leetho – is taken in and looked after. He is invited to the Phaeacian Games that are put on in his honour, where he surprises everyone, including himself, when he takes the prize for the discus.

Later, a banquet is thrown with Odysseus (Leetho) as the guest of honour. They are entertained by Demodocus, the bard, who goes on to regale them with many tales, one of which is a story unknown to the listeners, about how Odysseus tries to evade being sent to fight in the war. Leetho is incensed at Odysseus' behaviour, not knowing that it is his own. Demodocus finishes his tale with the story of the Wooden Horse of Troy (which happened nearly 20 years earlier, now!) When Odysseus hears this story being told to him, his memory suddenly returns and he weeps. When Alcinous sees him weeping he stops Demodocus and Odysseus explains who he is and continues the story to prove it. The authenticity of his account persuades them that he is telling the truth and Alcinous vows to do all he can to return Odysseus to his homeland. The following day Odysseus is escorted to Ithaca and this time he arrives there, only to be met by a mysterious woman (actually Athena, who is there to disguise him for the trials ahead).

Story

Odysseus was woken by the blinding light of the sun and though he was still alive, the trauma he had experienced had robbed him of his memory. As he came to, he could hear the sound of young people playing. He stood up and looked towards the source of the sound. When the children who were playing with a ball saw the strange figure rise up from the sand, they all scattered away in fear – all, that is, except for one fearless little girl. The dauntless youngster approached the dishevelled stranger and asked him directly, 'Who are you and why are you here?'

Figure 26: The dauntless youngster approached the dishevelled stranger.

'I'm ... nobody!' He scratched his head. 'I have forgotten who I am!' said Odysseus. The girl took Odysseus by the hand and said, 'Well, come with me and I'll take you to my father, King Alcinous – he will be able to help you. But before we go I must give you a name. "Nobody" won't do as a name at all. Mmm, let's see ... I know!' she exclaimed, following a thoughtful pause. 'You can be "Leetho" because you have forgotten yourself.' Leetho, in Ancient Greek means 'forget' or 'to escape one's notice'. Taking Odysseus by the hand, she marched the bemused man to her home.

The girl was called Nausicaa and she was afraid of no one. Nausicaa was the daughter of King Alcinous and Queen Arete who ruled the Phaeacians well. Odysseus had been washed up onto one of the many beautiful beaches of Phaeacia.

When she arrived at her father's palace, he was very surprised to see the stranger accompanying her. 'Who is this man that follows you like a drowned rat, my daughter?' asked Alcinous.

'He is called Leetho,' she said without any explanation, 'and I want you to give him a bath and some food and to make sure that he is properly looked after!'

King Alcinous looked at her, and, just as so many fathers of daughters all over the world do, he did exactly as he was told. So, *Leetho was washed, fed and rested. He was invited by King Alcinous to attend a games that would be put on in his honour, followed by a feast in the evening.*

Leetho was taken to the island's stadium for the games. The best athletes gathered to compete with each other in discus, javelin, wrestling, boxing, jumping and running races. Leetho watched with King Alcinous while the athletes competed. Once the games were finished, Laodamus, one of the best athletes, being also the son of King Alcinous, approached Leetho and challenged him to take part. Leetho did not know why but he felt utterly exhausted and too weak to compete so he turned down the offer. Laodamus took the opportunity to insult him, saying, 'You don't much look like an athlete anyway!' Angered by this, Leetho stood up and took the biggest discus of all, launching it through the air and sending it much further than the other athletes had been able to throw theirs. Laodamus and the other athletes were silenced. Leetho, too, was silenced as he was as surprised as they were. The prize for the discus was awarded to Leetho.

Memory and identity

You may want to use this PhiE to give the children time to work through the idea that Leetho and Odysseus are the same person, yet – in a way – different. But you may prefer not to fully explore the philosophical issues until you reach the second PhiE in this Chapter. This shorter discussion will then prime them for the more involved discussion later. But whether you follow the issues in depth here or later is up to you. Explore TQ 1 in order to answer TQ 2 more philosophically.

> TQ 1: Without any of Odysseus' memories is Leetho Odysseus or is Leetho a new person?

> TQ 2: So, who won the prize, Odysseus or Leetho?

Nested Questions

- Are they, Leetho and Odysseus, the same person?
- Socratic Question: What is a person?
- What makes a person the same person over time?
- How do you know that you are the same person you were
  a) a week ago?
  b) a year ago?
  c) five years ago?

d) when you were first born?

- a) Is memory important in deciding that you are the same person you were a year ago? b) If so, then without memories, would you be the same person you were a year ago?
- What do we mean when we say 'the same'?
- Are there different senses of 'the same person' here? (See Carve it up on page 16.)
- In the story, Odysseus is called Leetho while he has no memory. Is it right to call Odysseus 'Leetho' in the story, or should he still be called 'Odysseus'?

Story continued ...

That evening, after the games, Leetho sat at the banqueting table and ate well. Once the food had been served, singers and dancers were summoned by Alcinous for the entertainment of all. Then a blind old man called Demodocus was ushered into the hall. He carried a lyre under his arm and found his way with a wooden stick. The old man then began to tell stories.

After they had been regaled with many tales, some known and some unknown, Alcinous said, 'Tell our guest my favourite story, Demodocus: the one about the Wooden Horse of Troy and of the war between the Trojans and the Greeks. I love that tale!'

Laodamus stood and shouted out: 'Yes, tell us tales of brave Odysseus!'

Demodocus lifted his lyre and began to tell the tale, beginning with the abduction of Helen by Paris, then of the launching of a thousand ships, of the

Figure 27: Then a blind old man called Demodocus was ushered into the hall.

ten-year war and of the stalemate. Among the many tales Demodocus recounted, the following story was told near the beginning, and it is a story about Odysseus you haven't heard yet.

'When Menelaos married Helen,' said Demodocus, 'in the interests of peace, Odysseus advised the other suitors to refrain from aggressive actions following their bad feelings at having lost the hand of Helen in marriage. So instead of challenging or fighting Menelaos, the other suitors agreed to honour and protect Menelaos' marriage vows. Later, when Paris abducted Helen, Menelaos made the other suitors keep to their promise to aid him in retrieving his wife. Odysseus' advice had come back to haunt him. Soldiers were sent by Menelaos to round up a fighting force with which to attack the Trojans.

'When Menelaos' soldiers arrived to collect Odysseus, they found him ploughing a field wearing a funny hat, driving a horse and a donkey on his plough, even though one is supposed to plough using oxen. They also noticed that he was not sowing seeds but salt! The soldiers said that they were not going to be able to make use of Odysseus' famous resourcefulness in the war against the Trojans, because he was clearly quite mad. The leader, Palamedes, was cleverer than the others however, and he suspected that Odysseus was playing a trick on them, so he called for Penelope to bring her son Telemachus to him. Palamedes took the baby – for Telemachus was very young at that time – and placed the helpless infant in front of the plough, to test Odysseus' madness. Upon seeing his son about to be trampled, Odysseus seemed to find his senses again and leapt forward to pick up his baby. His trick to escape being enlisted to fight in the war had been exposed and he never forgave Palamedes for this. Odysseus later took his revenge on Palamedes during the Trojan War. He forged a letter to Palamedes, supposedly from the Trojan king Priam. The letter led to Palamedes being stoned to death as a traitor.'

When Leetho heard this story he stood up and shouted, 'This Odysseus should feel ashamed to have tried to escape being sent to war and for taking his revenge on poor Palamedes like that. If I were ever to find him, I would imprison him for his actions!'

Angered by Leetho's outburst, Laodamus replied, 'Sit down you insolent man! You know nothing of being Odysseus!'

'Before you condemn Odysseus, stranger,' said Demodocus to Leetho, 'let me finish the story. Odysseus had a reason for trying to escape the coming war: he had learned from the seer, Halitherses, that if he went to Troy he would not return for 20 years! So perhaps he was right to pretend to be mad.'

Eventually Demodocus reached the part when Odysseus thought up the strategy of the wooden horse to infiltrate the Trojan city and he told of how this led to the Trojan defeat.

'You see,' said Alcinous to Leetho, 'Odysseus is a real hero – if it weren't for his ingenuity, the Greeks would not have won the war. Were I ever to meet Odysseus I would honour him with great riches.' But Leetho did not reply. They saw that he was weeping.

Demodocus stopped his tale and said to the crying man, 'You're not supposed to weep yet! That bit comes later!' Alcinous lifted his hand and said, 'Stop the story here, Demodocus, and let our guest tell us why he is so moved.' They turned to hear Leetho's explanation.

'I weep, good King Alcinous,' he began, 'because this tale is known to me in a very different way to how it is known to you. When I found myself on your shores this morning I was confused by my last ordeal and I could not remember who I was, but the words of Demodocus have flown straight to my heart and have rekindled my memory. Suddenly all the tales are alive in me again.'

'What can you mean by this?' asked Alcinous 'Tell us: what is your name, sir?'

'I am ... Odysseus, son of Laertes – the Odysseus that you, Demodocus, have spoken of.'

'If you are indeed the resourceful king and warrior of the Horse of Troy,' said Alcinous, looking him up and down, 'then you certainly don't look anything like I would imagine the hero of these tales to look. Tell us your account; I want to know of your wanderings and where they have taken you since you left the shores of Troy – if you ever did! And then we can judge for ourselves whether you are indeed *the man you say you are.*'

Odysseus took a deep breath and began his tale. However, what Odysseus said will not be told again, as you have heard his tale already. Let me just say that the court of Alcinous marvelled at his ingenious escape from the cave of the Cyclops and wept at the encounter with his mother in the Underworld, and they grieved with Odysseus at the loss of his crew after they had angered Helios by slaughtering his sacred cows. And when he finally came to an end the following evening, there was a silence of many minutes after his finishing words, which were, '... and then your charming daughter, Nausicaa, gave me the name of Leetho, took me by the hand and led me to you, King Alcinous!'

After the silence, Alcinous said, 'I desire to know how the story ends but I now understand that it is not yet written. However, I will play my part willingly and without further obstacles to yourself. I shall provide you with a ship and with a crew to return you to your beloved land of Ithaca. You must leave tomorrow morning. Clearly, you are who you say you are, Odysseus, son of Laertes and *sacker of Troy. But I must ask you: now that you have met Odysseus, do you still wish to imprison him?'*

Odysseus turned to Alcinous with a wry smile and said, 'Now that you *have met him do you still wish to honour him?'*

Bravery and identity

There are two related philosophical enquiries here. One looks at the concept of bravery and its opposite, cowardice; the other discussion focuses on the philosophical problem of *personal identity over time*: what makes someone the same person through time? The topic of identity is continued in the next Chapter.

> TQ 3: Who is right? Should Odysseus be honoured or imprisoned?

Nested Questions
On bravery/cowardice

- Is Odysseus brave or a coward?
- Did Odysseus act in a cowardly way by pretending to be mad or do you think he had a good reason to try to escape being sent to war?
- Socratic Question: What is a coward?
- Socratic Question: What is bravery?

On identity and responsibility

- Is Leetho also responsible for the actions of Odysseus, that is to say, can he take credit for the idea of the wooden horse and should he be reproached for Odysseus' more questionable actions, when

  a) he has no memory of being Odysseus?
  b) he does have the memory of being Odysseus?

- Once his memory has returned, can Odysseus still lay claim to Leetho's prize for winning the discus?

  a) Given that you have no memory of being a baby, are you the same person now that you were when a baby? b) If so, what is it that makes you the same person over time?

Story continued …

'Indeed I do wish to honour him now that I have met Odysseus – or should I say, I do wish to honour you now that I have met you!' said Alcinous.

'The honour is all mine, however,' said Odysseus, 'to have met you, King Alcinous, and your delightful daughter. I am forever in your debt, especially Nausicaa's,' he finished.

Odysseus was given many gifts by Alcinous that amounted to the great riches he had promised. The gifts were loaded onto the ship and after making their farewells, Odysseus departed. The Phaeacians were consummate shipbuilders and sailors, so Odysseus was escorted swiftly and with great skill to ... well, let's see, shall we?

When the Phaeacian ship arrived at its destination, Odysseus was fast asleep and, so as not to disturb him, the crew lifted him gently from the ship and placed him, sleeping, on the beach. Then they unloaded his gifts and placed them next to him.

Eventually he awoke, somewhat confused, and surrounded by fog, the Phaeacian ship nowhere to be seen. He wondered to what island he had been brought, and whether he had been delivered to another unwelcoming island. Then the fog cleared and he noticed the familiar and imposing landmark of Mount Neriton, the mountain that overlooked the people of Ithaca, and he realised that he had finally been brought home.

Sadly, the ship that had delivered him, however, did not reach the shores of Phaeacia again. Poseidon was angry that they had escorted Odysseus to his homeland and so, just a mile short of Phaeacia, he turned the ship into stone. A rock in that place stands to this day off the coast of modern-day Corfu (thought to be the site of Phaeacia) and – to this day – is known by the locals as 'the ship of Odysseus'.

The mist's departure also revealed, standing before him, a mysterious woman who, upon seeing his approach, began to walk towards Odysseus. Who she was, he did not know. Was this to be yet another obstacle to his homecoming?

Extension Activity

Story of your life

Ask the pupils to write an account that describes, or 'tells', their life so far. You may want to set a word limit depending on their age. Alternatively, you may want to expand the exercise so that they start small and work out to a longer narrative. Can they tell their story in:

1 A word?
2 A phrase?
3 A sentence?
4 A paragraph?
5 A page? (etc.)

Or, through different media perhaps:

1 A poem?
2 An obituary? (depending on their age, of course)
3 A school report?
4 Or even *a song*?

14 The Stranger (The Return Home)

Philosophy

For dramatic and philosophical reasons I have made use of several devices for special effects in this, the last story. Firstly, the tenses are varied. To make a televisual analogy, the past tense is like watching something in black-and-white whereas the present tense is like watching in colour. I tell the 'meanwhile ...' section, which quickly brings the audience up to speed regarding the goings-on back in Ithaca, in the past tense, but then I switch to the present tense when we resume the story. This achieves a number of aims. It impresses the 'real-time' feel that I want the audience to be sensitive to. I also want the audience to *work with* the other characters – particularly Eumaeus, Telemachus and Penelope – in uncovering Odysseus' true identity. In my version, the audience have to earn the dramatic irony, usually given to them gratis. And very many of the children will know straight away that 'the stranger' is Odysseus, but others will take longer to work it out. Sometimes those that do know who he is suspend their disbelief and pretend not to know who he is in order to enter into the story.

The reason for this storytelling choice is that the theme of the accompanying PhiE session is *personal identity*, and this is based on the fact that Odysseus is in disguise in this story until the final climax. The audience begins by working with the supporting characters but then, at the end, they work with Odysseus to try to find a way to prove his true identity to the supporting characters.

It is worth noting that I have described the use of the above devices as 'storytelling choices' and it is, of course, up to you whether you make use of them too. As a storyteller you are in no way limited to using the tenses and dramatic devices I have used, but they act as suggestions and examples of just what you can do to 'ready-made' stories so that you can meet your – or the class's – pedagogical/dramatic/philosophical needs.

There is a further sense that we can draw philosophy from the themes of this story: the sense in which we are all 'strangers' to each other in that we are 'trapped' or 'confined' within our own subjectivity. We cannot know what someone else is thinking or feeling, and in fact, we cannot know for certain that other people even think or feel at all – for all you know, everyone else could be a kind of *zombie*, acting *as though* they have thoughts and feelings but having no such corresponding experiences in their brains. The '*hidden-ness*' of other minds becomes highlighted when, for instance, we have to try to ascertain whether someone is being sincere or not. We can only surmise from outward displays of facial expressions or from what we know of their characters – we cannot know 'from the inside'.

In my version of this story I have toned down the violence – at least my description of it – for primary school audiences. You may deem it appropriate to reinstate the original ending for older students, as it provides yet another perfect opportunity to discuss the ethics of Odysseus against a backdrop of differing values from our own (see The Ciconians, The Laestrygonians and the accompanying online supplement When in Rome ... for more on this). In the original, Odysseus, Telemachus and Eumeaus kill all the suitors in a battle and then they hang all the disloyal maids, sparing only the faithful ones. There are some further even more gruesome details: the disloyal maids are made to carry the corpses of their dead lovers before they are hung, and a character called Melanthius is horribly dismembered for helping the suitors during the battle. I have also taken out altogether a battle following the reunion between Odysseus' house and some friends of the suitors.

Storykit
Names to learn in this story

- **Eumaeus** (You-**may**-us): An old servant of Odysseus, now an exiled shepherd.
- **Pylos** (**Py**-los): City on the west coast of the Peloponnese (now part of Greece) and home of Nestor.
- **Sparta** (**Spa**-ta): Home of Menelaos and Helen, also in the Peloponnese.
- **Nestor** (**Nes**-tor): King of Pylos.
- **Antinous** (**An**-tin-us): The leader of the suitors.
- **Argus** (**Ar**-gus): Odysseus' old hunting dog.
- **Eurycleia** (Yoo-ri-**cla**-ya): Odysseus' old nurse.

Keyword list

- Meanwhile in Ithaca ... (20 years!).
- After age 17: 108 suitors (Antinous).
- Telemachus leaves.
- The tapestry trick.
- Telemachus: Pylos and Sparta (Nestor and Menelaos).
- Ambush! Athena helps.
- Back to the story ...
- The three of them.
- (The Liar's Paradox).
- The stranger and the message.
- The two men.
- To the palace.
- Argus, the old dog.
- Announcement.
- The stranger and Penelope.
- Eurycleia and the scar.
- The 12 axes.
- Telemachus, Suitors, Antinous all fail.
- (Lock up).
- The stranger's turn.
- Censored!
- Suitors gone.
- Penelope's disbelief.
- The wedding bed.
- Reunited.
- Immortality after all!

Storykit Hint: Telling the story differently (Can you step in the same story twice?)

A good storyteller never tells the same story in exactly the same way. Of course, when they have told a story many times, much of it will be the same, but because they have not learned the story line by line, they have an enormous amount of freedom denied the actor in a play, for instance, or the reader of a book, or the reciter of a poem. Storytellers can tell a story the same way if they want to, but they can also change it to suit their audience, or to suit the time of day, the mood they are in, or they may change it just for fun! Often a teller likes to experiment to see if changing the tense, for example, will make it better, or reversing the sequence of events, and so on. Try out different ways of telling your stories and use your audience to gauge whether they should be changes you keep.

Synopsis for The Stranger (The Return Home)

Odysseus makes his way, disguised by Athena as a stranger from Crete, to the hut of Eumaeus, his old, faithful servant. After sailing the seas in search of his father, Telemachus is also sent by Athena to the hut of Eumaeus. Penelope has finally come to the end of weaving a tapestry that she has been secretly unpicking in order to delay marriage to one of the suitors, so she can stall no more. The three men all meet at the hut but Odysseus remains disguised until Eumaeus is sent on to the city to tell Penelope of her son's return, at which point Odysseus reveals his true identity to Telemachus. The two of them hatch a plan, and then Telemachus, Eumaeus and Odysseus head to the palace. When they arrive, Odysseus is recognised by his old hunting dog, Argus – presumably by his scent – but the excitement kills the dog.

Penelope announces that there will be a competition to fire an arrow from Odysseus' special hunting bow through an alignment of axes: the winner will become her next husband. The stranger (Odysseus) meets Penelope and tells her that he has news of Odysseus and that he is alive. The stranger is washed by Eurycleia and she recognises a wound Odysseus received as a boy, but she remains silent. Nobody has the strength to string the bow until the 'stranger from Crete' is allowed to try. Odysseus strings it and then turns it against the suitors. Telemachus, Eumeaus and Odysseus kill all the suitors and traitors. Penelope refuses to believe that the stranger is Odysseus until he proves his identity to her by his knowledge of a hidden olive tree built into the frame of their wedding bed. All are finally – and joyfully – reunited.

Story

It is at this point in the story that you need to know what has been happening in Ithaca during the time that Odysseus has been away.

Twenty years earlier, Odysseus set sail with the other Greek ships to bring back Helen. He and his men didn't expect to be away for very long, maybe a few months at the most. He had instructed Penelope to remarry only if their son, Telemachus, would come of age before Odysseus' return.

After 17 years of Ithaca having no king, a marauding host of suitors – 108 to be precise – descended on the palace demanding that Penelope take a new husband, so that one of the suitors could become king of Ithaca. Despite Telemachus' attempts to stop them, they moved into the palace and took up residence there, eating the food and drinking the wine and spending the money that was meant for Telemachus.

Figure 28: Despite Telemachus' attempts to stop them, they moved into the palace and took up residence there.

Odysseus' son was visited by the goddess Athena who advised him to leave Ithaca and travel abroad to seek news of his father. He took her advice and left without a word, leaving his mother devastated at the news of her son's departure.

Under pressure from the suitors, Penelope reluctantly agreed that she would remarry when she had completed a tapestry she was making for her husband. However, she had a plan to delay a remarriage. Each night, after she had spent a day's work on the tapestry, she crept down to it and unpicked much of what she had done that day. This meant that she took much longer to complete the tapestry and thereby delayed having to take a new husband. And in the farthest reaches of her heart she still retained a glimmer of hope that her true husband might yet return before she remarried.

Telemachus, in the meantime, visited some old friends of Odysseus in Pylos and Sparta, including Nestor and Menelaos, both of whom were with him in Troy, Menelaos being the husband of Helen – the woman with 'the face that launched a thousand ships'. Telemachus learned very little of Odysseus after he had left Troy, though he managed to work out that his father might still be alive as no one had reported his death.

Whilst Telemachus was away, the suitors, who were headed by one called Antinous, had planned, upon his return, to kill Odysseus' son in an ambush. Eventually, Telemachus was told to return to Ithaca by Athena but she also advised him against returning to the palace right away because of the ambush.

She told him, instead, to go to the hut of Eumaeus, an old and faithful servant of Odysseus, who had been banished from the palace by the suitors.

We can now return to our story ...

When Telemachus eventually arrives at the hut of Eumaeus – now a shepherd – he is greeted warmly by the old man, but discovers that Eumaeus is not alone. 'Who is this strange beggar that sits and eats at your table?' asks Telemachus, looking over Eumaeus' shoulder.

'This is a traveller from Crete,' explains Eumaeus. 'He says that he needs to deliver a message to the palace of Penelope and Telemachus. He has been asking all kinds of questions concerning the goings-on at the palace but he seems friendly enough.'

Telemachus looks suspiciously at the stranger. He looks old and grey-haired, weak, dirty and undernourished. Telemachus whispers to Eumaeus, 'You know what they say about Cretans, don't you? That even they call themselves liars!'

Telemachus asks Eumaeus to go to the palace to inform Penelope of his return. While Eumaeus is away, the stranger from Crete reveals one of his messages to Telemachus that brings joy to both their hearts. After embracing, the two of them sit down and hatch a plan together.

Later that day, when Eumaeus has returned, the three of them decide to head to the palace. Before they enter, they send Telemachus through the gates first while the stranger and Eumaeus follow. Telemachus is reunited with his mother and their meeting is most tearful because she is pleased to see her son again, but she also knows that she must marry one of the dreadful suitors the very next day.

Immediately upon entering the palace grounds, the stranger – who looks and smells like a beggar – begins to receive abuse from the suitors that litter the courtyard. Perhaps because of his beggar-like appearance, he is kicked, insulted and spat upon.

Curled up in the corner of the courtyard, barely awake, is Argus, Odysseus' favourite hunting dog. He is now very old and grey as it has been some 20 years since he last went hunting with his master.

Upon hearing a commotion, the old dog slowly glances round to see the stranger. Argus sniffs the air and then his tail begins to wag. He gets up and with what little strength he still has he makes his way, limping, over to the stranger. His tail wags more vigorously the closer he gets.

The old dog appears to be overjoyed to see the beggar, much to the consternation of the suitors who look on quizzically as the dog licks the stranger's face. The excitement, however, is too much for the old dog and his heart gives way

Figure 29: Curled up in the corner of the courtyard, barely awake, is Argus.

while he is held in the stranger's arms. The stranger wipes away a single tear from his face. He looks round, hoping that nobody saw his tear, while Argus lies dead in his arms.

At that moment, Penelope emerges from the palace and everyone in the courtyard stops to listen. Today is the day that she can no longer play her trick. The tapestry is finally completed and so she announces, with a downhearted tone, that she will take a new husband the next day. She explains that there will be a competition and whoever is able to string Odysseus' hunting bow and shoot through 12 axes will achieve her hand in marriage. Everyone hears this, including Eumaeus and the stranger. Without a further word and with her head bowed low, she goes back inside.

Telemachus enters the palace building and introduces the stranger to Penelope and she asks him who the stranger is. Telemachus says: 'He is a stranger from Crete who has requested an audience with you, my dearest mother. He says he has a message for you though he won't tell me what it is. I brought him here so that he may tell you.'

'So, Cretan!' instructs Penelope, 'tell me your message!'

The stranger speaks with a heavy Cretan accent. 'I have a message from ... Odysseus, your husband: he told me to tell you that he is alive and that he will soon return.'

'This cannot be!' she says. 'How can you know of him?'

'I have met him on my travels,' says the stranger.

Penelope is visibly moved, though she stops any tears from falling. She turns to her nurse, Eurycleia, and, perceiving that the stranger is unclean, she tells her faithful nurse to wash him. Penelope does this in gratitude for the news of Odysseus that he has brought her, though she does not believe it.

Like Eumeaus and Argus, Eurycleia had served the family for many years. She had washed Odysseus often as a boy and there was something that had happened to him as a boy when he was out hunting one day. During the hunt he had been gored by a wild boar. This left a deep scar on his thigh. In a few moments she would be reminded of this distant memory.

While Eurycleia is washing the stranger she sees a distinguishing mark that makes her gasp. She is just about to get up to tell her mistress what she has seen when she catches sight of the stranger looking at her intently, his index finger gently crossing his mouth in a gesture of quiet. She sits back down, not quite able to believe what it is she suspects she has discovered.

Penelope has the axes and bow brought into the main chamber where the competition is to take place. Telemachus arranges the 12 axes in a neat row in front of a wooden post. The axes are double-headed and the task is to send an arrow from Odysseus' bow straight through the narrow passage that lies through the tops of the aligned axe-heads to skewer the post at the end.

The bow is not strung, so, before the competition can begin, it needs to be restrung. This is done by attaching the string to one end of the bow and then bending the wood so that the other end of the string can be looped around the other end of the bow. It will take an enormous amount of strength to do this. Telemachus tries to string the bow first, and, though he is nearly able to do so, it is too much for him. Several of the other suitors follow him in the attempt but they fail abysmally. Antinous, the leader of the suitors, tries last of all. He does best of all the suitors but is still not able to bend the bow enough to string it.

While all this is going on, the stranger has a quiet word in the ear of Eumeaus. The old man looks shocked and joyful at the same time at whatever news the stranger has whispered to him. Whatever it was that the stranger told him, Eumeaus discretely moves to the doors and then locks and bars them. He then escorts Penelope and her faithful servants to her bedchamber.

When Antinous is unable to string the bow, Telemachus stands up and says, 'Why not let the Cretan have a go?' pointing to the stranger next to him.

'The beggar?!' exclaims Antinous. He stares at the weak, old beggar and then says, 'He'll never do it!'

'Well, if he'll never do it,' says Telemachus, 'then it won't harm to let him try and humiliate himself with the rest of us, will it?'

'*Very well,*' *agrees Antinous at length.*

The stranger steps forward and takes the bow from him – the bow that only Odysseus was ever able to wield. The stranger takes the string in one hand and begins to put his weight on the bow. Quickly and smoothly – and to the astonishment of all the suitors – he succeeds in stringing it; he lifts the bow and shoots the arrow clean through the tops of the axes and into the centre of the pole.

Meanwhile, Telemachus and Eumaeus have armed themselves, and the stranger turns his bow, and his wrath, towards the suitors …

I am afraid that you – the audience – will also have to be left, with Penelope and her maids, in the bedroom, because the scene that unfolds in the main chamber is not a scene that should be described in detail. Let's just say that the suitors would give the palace no more trouble from that day on!

*When all the suitors and traitors have finally been '*dealt with*', the stranger is taken with Telemachus, Eumaeus and Eurycleia to Penelope, who is herself shocked at this very unexpected turn of events. '*Who is this stranger from Crete who has caused so much trouble for my tormentors and who has done what none of us could achieve?*' she demands from them all.*

*It is Eurycleia who answers first: '*My lady, the man who has come to us unkempt and unclean, I believe* is *your husband, Odysseus, though I do not recognise his face.*'

'*Odysseus?!*' shouts the Queen. '*But I would recognise my own husband if he stood before me, would I not?*'

*Telemachus speaks to her next: '*I believe *also that this is my father.*'

'*This* is *Odysseus,*' *reinforces Eumaeus, confirming the claims of both Telemachus and Eurycleia.*

*Then it comes to the stranger's turn to speak: '*I have laboured long to be here, but the reason why you do not recognise me, my lovely Penelope, is because, when I arrived on the shores of Ithaca just two days ago, I was met by Athena, who gave me the visage of a stranger and a beggar to aid my secret return. She advised me to first of all visit the hut of Eumaeus, which I did, and where I first laid eyes on my grown-up son. On my honour, beneath this repulsive exterior I truly am* Odysseus.'

*Penelope looks at him in disbelief. '*This cannot be true!*' she says. '*If I am to believe you then you must prove it, otherwise I cannot put my heart in jeopardy by allowing hope to spring up where it has lain stifled and stopped for so long. It would kill me if I believed you and it turned out to be false.*'

Personal identity

> TQ: Given that Athena has completely changed Odysseus' physical appearance, how can Odysseus prove that he is Odysseus?

Nested Questions

- If your physical appearance is completely changed then are you the same person?
- If your physical appearance is completely changed then how might other people know that you are the same person? Or can they?
- What is it that makes you the same person?
- Are there any features or qualities that you can't change without making you into someone else? (See the teaching strategy 'Sine Qua Non' in *The If Machine* on page 45.)
- How did Argus know that the stranger was Odysseus? Did Argus really know?
- How did Eurycleia know that the stranger was Odysseus? Did Eurycleia really know?

Story continued ...

'Your bed!' says the stranger, unexpectedly, 'It has within it a secret known only to yourself and your husband. If I can tell you that secret then I must be your husband, must I not?'

'Go on,' permits Penelope.

'It was built on your wedding day, by your husband, over an olive tree that is now hidden under its frame,' reveals the stranger.

Disbelief finally gives way to belief as Penelope's gaze becomes blurred with tears. 'My husband, come to me after all this time and hold me, my dear, truthful Odysseus.'

As she finally allows hope back into her heart, the stranger begins to change as Athena's magic fades, though Penelope can no longer see him through her tears. Instead, she takes him in her arms and lavishes him with kisses of joy and welcome and love, all of which have slept in her for far too long. The true king of Ithaca is home at last.

Epilogue

When Tiresias had looked into Odysseus' future from the vantage point of death, what he had seen, in addition to Odysseus' many adventures at sea, was that he would meet a gentle death at the close of a very respectable old age. But in the telling – and retelling – of this story Odysseus achieves the immortality Kalypso had promised him if only he would stay with her; and he did so in spite of not having stayed with her, because Odysseus lives on with each telling of his tale. To keep him alive, keep telling the tale of his *Odyssey*!

Section 3
After The *Odyssey*

Appendix 1: The Hero

Figure 30: Odysseus the hero?

Philosophy

A hero in the time of Homer was very different from a hero in later history. Then, a hero was high-born and embodied virtues such as strength and courage, what might be called 'battlefield virtues'. In this regard it is worth noting that the word 'hero' comes from the Greek *heros* (pronounced **heh**-ross), which means 'defender, protector'. The heroes of Greek myth (e.g. Achilles, Heracles, Theseus, Perseus and, of course, Odysseus) were also often selfish, arrogant and without the virtues that would typify a hero in post-Christian times.

The German philosopher, Nietzsche, thought that this transformation didn't occur with the advent of Jesus but with Socrates who, he thought, was the first to advocate the moral virtues such as self-sacrifice, humility, subservience to truth, and so on, over strength and prowess on the battlefield. These days, you can find heroes of both sorts: from the action hero, such as Batman, James Bond, Buffy the Vampire Slayer, to the moral hero, such as Schindler,

Superman, George Bailey in *It's a Wonderful Life*, Arthurian knights, and so on. Just spend some time listing how many of each you can think of. Which list is easier to fill? It seems that most examples of the latter are to be found in history rather than in fiction (e.g. Gandhi, Socrates, Jesus), although the extent to which the characters of these stories are fictional embellishments on historical figures is interesting in itself.

The question whether Odysseus is a hero, or a good man, is a question that can be found threaded throughout the stories of the *Odyssey*. That is why I like to come to this question at the *end* of the *Odyssey*. The children will have heard how he was willing to sacrifice himself to save his men from Circe, but they will also have heard how his hubristic pride brought on the wrath of Poseidon, a move that would endanger the crew. They will have been puzzled as to why he didn't attempt to save his crew but only himself when the ship was sunk by Zeus, and they may have considered his heroic attempt to return his men to Ithaca an abject failure given that they all died. Yet they will have been impressed at how his ingenuity often served him and his crew well.

By ancient or modern standards, the question as to whether Odysseus was a hero is a complicated one, and one that the class would do well to consider. What adds to his complexity is the fact that the character of Odysseus is a composite of many different authors from Homer to Euripides and Sophocles, each one portraying many of the same events but with a different angle, portraying him from heroic to roguish. Yet this only goes to show the complexity of any identity drawn from narratives, because one's own story has to be understood in the light of other's versions of the same story. Different people see the same events differently.

The Hero

The Task Questions for this section should be as follows:

TQ 1: Was Odysseus a hero?
TQ 2: Was Odysseus a good man?

Nested Questions

- Socratic Question: What is a hero?
- Are there different kinds of hero?
- Socratic Question: What is a good person?
- Is a hero the same as a good person?
- Can a hero be a bad person?

- Can a hero be flawed?
- Who is your hero? Why are they your hero?

A further important discussion for this section could also be:

TQ 3: Was Odysseus a good leader?

Nested Questions

- Socratic Question: What is a good leader?
- Can a good leader fail?
- Does a good leader always make the right decisions?

Here are some choice scenes from the *Odyssey* to refer to when answering these questions, though the children may well refer to other scenes not listed here:

- Odysseus the madman (as told by Demodocus). Page 141
- His devising of the wooden horse plan in the Trojan war. Page 30
- His advice to kill Astyanax (see below for this story).
- His attack on the Ciconians. Page 35
- His protection of Maron the Ciconian priest. Page 36
- His resistance of the juice of the Lotus Eaters. Page 44
- His ingenious escape from the island of the Cyclops. Page 51
- His declaration to Polyphemus of who he really is. Page 54
- His promise to return his crew home after the mutiny. Page 66
- His decision to try to retrieve his men from Circe. Page 82
- His actions passing the Sirens and then Scylla and Charybdis. Page 98 and 110
- Saving himself after the ship is sunk by Zeus. Page 123
- His resistance to Kalypso's offers. Page 131
- The winning of the discus prize. Page 139
- His treatment of the suitors (and disloyal servants). Page 147 and 154

Advanced Extension Activity

(Suitable for older students only)

Once the Greeks had tricked their way into the city walls of Troy using Odysseus' clever plan to hide inside a giant wooden horse, among the people of Troy found by the Greeks inside the city was a child called Astyanax (pronounced as-**ty**-a-nax). Astyanax was the baby boy of the now dead hero of the Trojans, Hektor, one of the sons of King Priam. Odysseus advised the Greeks to kill Astyanax as he feared that if they did not, he would later, as a man, seek to avenge his father. The Greeks agreed with Odysseus and so Astyanax was murdered, though not by Odysseus. He was dropped from the top of the tallest tower in Troy by Neoptolemus (pronounced nee-op-**toh**-le-mus).

Note: There are some extremely moving passages in the *Iliad*, also by Homer (6.466–74, 6.467–81, 24.725–37), and Euripides' *The Trojan Women* (749–60, 1173–93) that describe the event of Astyanax's death and its effects on other characters in the story. (References taken from the *Dictionary of Classical Mythology* by Jenny March.)

Related thought experiments (also for older students only):

- Would it be morally right to kill a baby if he or she was going to commit terrible acts as an adult? (For example, Hitler.)
- Would what you know about the situation make a difference?
- Would it be morally right to kill a baby Hitler if you did not know what he was going to grow up to do?
- Would it be morally right to kill a baby Hitler if you did know what he was going to grow up to do?
- See online supplement to this chapter Moral and Prudential Goods, and also see online supplement for Chapter 6: When in Rome ... (The Laestrygonians) for a discussion of relativism/absolutism.

Appendix 2: Introduction to Ancient Greek

Our Hero

Before beginning the stories, and only if you are planning to do the course in Ancient Greek with the children, begin by writing the word 'Odysseus' in Ancient Greek. This can either be done by writing it on the board like so, O δ υ σ σ ε υ ς, or, you can write each letter on a piece of A4 paper, nice and big, and have them scattered randomly in the centre of the floor. I recommend you practise writing them yourself beforehand, if you are going to teach them.

The children then have to try to ascertain the following bits of information through questioning you. You should try to get them to answer all these questions with educated guesses and a few clues from yourself:

- What are these symbols? (They make a word.)
- Why are they here? (To *transliterate*. Explain the difference between this and 'translation'.)
- What language are they from? (Ancient Greek.)
- What country is the language from? (Greece.)
- What English letter does each symbol correspond to? (Literally: 'O', 'd', 'u', 's', 's', 'e', 'u', 's'.)
- What does it mean? (It is the name of the main protagonist of the *Odyssey*, Odysseus. Once they have transliterated it they may guess this.)

Rules of Ancient Greek and possible points of confusion that you must be aware of for this activity:

- When translating we replace some – but not all – 'u's with a 'y'. The word 'Odysseus' has both kinds of 'u' – one we replace with a 'y' and one we don't.
- An 's' at the beginning or middle of a word is written 'σ' but if an 's' ends a word then it looks like this: 'ς'.

If using the board, then, once you are ready to begin with the transliteration, write numbers 1 to 8 above the symbols for ease of reference, like so:

1 2 3 4 5 6 7 8
Ο δ υ σ σ ε υ ς

If using the paper method, then get them to write, on a piece of A4, the English letters they think go with the Greek letters and have them place these letters below the Greek. I ask them to do this in pairs where they both have to agree, between them, what the corresponding English letter is. Ask other members of the class to correct any matches they don't think are correct.

'Philosophy'

A similar activity can be done with the word 'philosophy' though you may prefer to do these two activities at different times, making sure they are both done before you reach the Ancient Greek Workshop (see Appendix 3):

1 2 3 4 5 6 7 8 9
φ ι λ ο σ ο φ ι α

Begin the second activity by getting the class to spell 'philosophy' in English on the board first, so that they have something to compare with when transliterating. Say it in clear, phonetic syllables to help them with the spelling: 'fih-loh-soh-fee-ya'. The aim of this activity is to place the symbols in the correct order.

Here are some further Greek points to be aware of that may cause confusion:

- The single phi symbol φ captures two English symbols, 'ph', but only one sound, 'fuh'.
- The translation changes the last two letters of the transliteration 'i' and 'a' into one letter: 'y' (as in 'Italia' to 'Italy').

See if you can find a way to get the children to solve these problems for themselves. For instance, they will often try to find an 'h' for the second letter. If they try to do this, then ask them what they think the second letter is. If they say 'h', then say, 'The second letter is not an 'h', though that is a very good guess. So, if it's not an 'h', what do you think the second letter will be?' You could also ask them why they think it is not an 'h'. Or you could ask this at the end.

Let them know that some of the letters are very obvious but others are not so obvious, so make sure they know that they don't have to do them in order.

That way you should encourage them to do the easy ones first. A process of elimination should then aid them with the harder ones.

A starting definition of 'philosophy'

Once they have translated 'philosophy', explain that it is made of two words in Ancient Greek, 'philo' and 'sophia', and that *philo* means *love* or *friendship* ('love' as in 'when you *love* doing something like football or drawing'), and that *sophia* means *wisdom* or *learning*. So, all together, it means 'love of wisdom' or 'friendship of learning'. This means that a philosopher is someone who loves learning, thinking and exploring ideas, but it also means that they like to learn, think and explore ideas with other people and not just on their own. Before saying all this you could do *Break the circle* (see page 15) on *wisdom*.

Here is the Ancient Greek alphabet (upper and lower case) complete with pronunciation guide:

Name	Upper	Lower	Pronunciation
Alpha	A	α	a as in father
Beta	B	β	b as in English
Gamma	Γ	γ	g hard, as in get
Delta	Δ	δ	d as in English
Epsilon	E	ε	e as in set
Zeta	Z	ζ	'sd' as in wisdom
Eta	H	η	e long, as in hair
Theta	Θ	θ	th as in thin
Iota	I	ι	i as in hit
Kappa	K	κ	k as in English
Lambda	Λ	λ	l as in English
Mu	M	μ	m as in English
Nu	N	ν	n as English
Xi	Ξ	ξ	x as in English
Omicron	O	ο	o as in hot
Pi	Π	π	p as in English
Rho	P	ρ	r as in English
Sigma	Σ	σ (or ς)	s as in sister
Tau	T	τ	t as in English
Upsilon	Y	υ	oo as in too
Phi	Φ	φ	ph as in philosophy
Chi	X	χ	ch as in loch
Psi	Ψ	ψ	ps as in lapse
Omega	Ω	ω	au as in caught

Appendix 3: Ancient Greek Workshop

This workshop takes either an entire morning or an entire afternoon. Alternatively, you could spread it over several sessions, doing one activity each time. It is best approached when the children have already completed the tasks in Appendix 2 to translate 'Odysseus' and 'philosophy'. That way they already have a knowledge of some symbols, and it is probably better to remind them (or have them remind themselves) of what they learnt in those two tasks before beginning the workshop.

The pedagogical principle that underpins this workshop is what you might call *scaffolding*. That is to say, the workshop has been carefully put together so that the children can work out the new information at each stage. The teacher should refrain from giving answers as much as possible to encourage the children to teach themselves.

There are a few exceptions where the teacher may need to teach, such as the rule that the 's' (ς) in Ancient Greek is different at the end of words from the 's' at the beginning or in the middle of words (σ). It is still possible for them to work this out if you question them well, making use of information they may already have gleaned. For instance, when you come to 'eureka' they are likely to say that the third letter ρ is a 'p', as it looks like one. However, they should notice, with or without prompting from the teacher, that they have already done a 'p' earlier in 'Oidipous' and that the 'p' was the *pi* symbol π. If they do need prompting then here's a good prompter-question: 'Is there anything already on the board that can help you with this?' You could suggest that they complete the rest of the word, the remaining letters of which should be familiar, and then return to the unknown symbol ρ. If they spot the English word, *eureka*, then they are likely to be able to work out that it is an 'r'.

There should be a similar way that you can get the children to teach themselves what the unfamiliar symbols are in each new word, using a combination of previous knowledge, elimination and educated guessing. Once they have been reminded of the symbols that they already know from the words 'Odysseus' and 'philosophy', then proceed through the following stages of the workshop:

1 *Spot the hero*: Before you begin the story, write up and number each letter as you did for 'Odysseus' and 'philosophy' (see Appendix 2):

1 2 3 4 5 6 7 8

Ο ι δ ι π ο υ ς

2 When you reach the riddles and you stop the story, have the children transliterate the word on the board, identifying which English letter goes under each Greek letter. As with the earlier, similar tasks, encourage them to do the obvious ones first such as 'o', 'i', 'u' and 's', leaving 'd' and 'p' until last. When (and *if*) they think they know what the word is, then they can work out what 'pi' stands for. If they don't, then teach it to them. The transliteration is 'Oidipous' but the translation I have opted for is 'Oidipus'.

3 *Guess the pair*:

(a) Write up, only in ancient Greek symbols, the following words: 'elephas' (ελεφας), 'idea' (ιδεα), 'Olympic' (Ολυμπια), 'balle' (βαλλε).

(b) Ask them to transliterate and to guess what English words they correspond to. These words are Ancient Greek words and have been chosen especially because they are so similar to their English equivalents. It helps to really illustrate to children how much of our language is of Ancient Greek origin.

(c) To help with the latter task (especially for the younger ones), you could write up the English words in a different order on the opposite side of the board so that their job is to find the corresponding pairs:

- ιδεα = idea
- βαλλε = throw (hint: say: 'It's not a ball, though that is a good guess; *balle* is the Ancient Greek for … Here's a clue: what do you *do* with a ball?')
- ελεφας = elephant
- Ολυμπια = Olympic

4 *Looking for 'phi'* (φ): Explain that there are many words in English that come from Ancient Greek words like the ones above, but if they want a quick way to find English words that come from Ancient Greek then suggest that they look for words that have a 'ph' for a 'fuh' sound. Ask them to list as many as they can. You are likely to hear, 'phone', which means 'sound' and is part of 'telephone' where 'tele' means 'distant' so together it makes 'distant-sound'.

This is a good opportunity to explain that many Greek words are often two smaller words put together to make bigger ones (there are English equivalents that you could ask them to pick out such as 'sunhat' or 'fireman'). Other words you are likely to hear are: 'physical' (phusis = nature); 'photo' (light); 'television' – which may get a mention when you say 'telephone' (tele = 'distant', as before, but 'vision' actually comes from the Latin for 'to see', so it is an interesting mixture of Greek *and* Latin origins, which is fairly common in English). 'Philosophy' may of course come up (philo = love and sophia = wisdom), and it is a good example of a longer word made of two smaller ones. Don't worry about words you don't know the origins for – these make excellent 'research words' for the class. Make a list such as this:

- Telephone
- Photogenic
- Graph
- Geography
- Biography
- Autobiography
- Telegraph
- Monograph

5 (Optional) *Ancient Greek Boggle*: Boggle is a game where you have a random selection of 16 letters and you have to find as many words as you can using the letters. Using any selection of the Greek words you have on the board, such as *idea, balle, oidipous, elephas* and *olumpia*, give them a time limit, such as five minutes, to find as many English words as they can but using the Greek symbols, so λ, ε, α, π spells 'leap', and σ, ε, λ, λ spells 'sell', and so on. Get them to do this activity in pairs or small groups. You could make this competitive.

6 *Ancient Greek words*: It is important to introduce the words in the order I've presented them here as each word has been chosen to borrow most letters from the ones already known but to introduce something new, usually not so obvious, for them to work out. Have them transliterate each word and then have them try to work out what they think the word is:

(a) β ι β λ ο ς (*book* as in 'bible' which simply means 'book')
(b) σ κ ο π (*look* as in 'scope')

(c) τ ε λ ε (*distant*. Encourage them to put this together with another word on the board to make a familiar English word: 'telescope'.)

(d) ε υ ρ η κ α (*Eureka!* as in 'I've got it!' Literally: 'I have found [it]!')

(e) π α ρ α δ ε ι σ ο ς (*garden* in Greek but more familiar as 'paradise' in English, probably from the biblical paradise, the garden of Eden.)

(f) π ε ρ ι ('around' as in '*perimeter*'. Encourage them to put this together with another word already on the board to make an English word to do with submarines: 'periscope'.)

(IMPORTANT: 7 and 8 should not be done until you have read or told the story Winged Words (App. 4) to the class and reached the point where the riddles are found by Oidipus.)

7 *Translate the coded riddles*: Hand out the Winged Words worksheets (online) to the children, in either pairs or groups, for them to try to complete. They should look at the riddles first, then use the Ancient Greek alphabet to transliterate, and then write down what they think is the English letter onto the 'Transliteration' sheets. There is one tricky bit where the 'theta' (θ), though only one letter in Greek, will need two letters, 't' and 'h', in English to make the singular sound 'th'. You could explain this or allow some of the children to figure it out and then give them the job of going around the class to explain this to the others. Either give both riddles to all the groups/pairs or divide the riddles up so that half the children do one riddle and the other half do the other.

8 *Solve the Sphinx's riddles*: Once the riddles have been decoded, the next task is to see if the children can solve the riddles. It is quite likely that there will be some children that have heard the first of the two riddles. Ask anyone who knows it to refrain from saying anything until the others have had a go. You could always ask those that know the riddle to think of a clue to give the others to help them. It is not essential that the children solve the riddles. What is essential is that they break the code in order for the story to continue.

Appendix 4: Winged Words (Oidipus and The Riddle of The Sphinx)

Philosophy

There are several riddles in this story. There are the two riddles spoken by the Sphinx and asked of all her victims, the first of which, The Creature, is very well known. I have not yet come across a class of children where at least one of them had not heard the first of the two riddles before, in one form or another. The second of the two riddles, The Sisters, is not so well known but was apparently included in some tellings of the story. I have included them both, for fun, and for more transliteration opportunities. The third riddle is a philosophical riddle and although brought out here by the author, it is a puzzle that is riddled throughout Greek mythology: that of how to make sense of the often whimsical way in which the gods threw obstacles in the way of the human characters. I have symbolised this with the use of the goddess *Tyche*, justified, I think, because the various versions of the story have different gods send the Sphinx. And, for reasons of simplicity, I have omitted the complex reasons given for the gods punishing the Thebans, making it, in this case, a random, reasonless event. Given this amendment, I thought it right to appeal to the appropriate deity. Tyche is the goddess of chance events. This also allows for the philosophical issues surrounding *chance* to make an appearance.

Using the Ancient Greek Workshop

If you use the story to frame the Ancient Greek Workshop, then tell the story until Oidipus finds the parchment – at which point stop the story and give out the Winged Words worksheets available online. Take them through the workshop plan in Appendix 3, the last activity of which is to transliterate the riddles. They are in English but with Greek symbols, so it is an exercise in relating the Greek symbols to the English ones. Once they have transliterated the riddles, spend some time trying to solve them. Like Oidipus, you may want to help them by giving clues to help overcome the metaphors 'in the morning', 'in the afternoon', and so on.

Figure 31: Tyche, goddess of chance events

Storykit
Names to learn in this story

- **Oidipus** (**oi**-di-pus – I have stuck to the phonetic pronunciation, as opposed to the usual **ee**-di-pus, to help with transliteration): Oidipus is one of the great Greek heroes but who comes to a tragic end in the canonical versions of his story – he unknowingly kills his father and marries his mother, fathering four children by her, only to gouge out his eyes and wander off into the wilderness when he realises what he has done. He typifies the human who is utterly ruined by the unseen outcomes of fate, and therefore a fitting hero for association with Tyche.
- **Tyche** (**ti**-kay): Goddess of fortune, luck and chance. Her Roman counterpart, *Fortuna*, is more familiar. She was invoked to account for unexplained events, particularly calamities. Both Tyche and Fortuna were often depicted standing on the wheel of fortune, holding in one hand a cornucopia, symbolising what fortune can give in one's favour, and in the other hand, a ship's rudder, showing how quickly and unexpectedly she may change one's fortune from good to bad or from bad to good.
- **Sphinx** (**sfinx**): A mythical creature with one foot in the mythology of several civilisations, and is probably best known in her Egyptian form. In contrast to the Greek depiction, the Egyptians depicted the Sphinx as benevolent and male.
- **Thebes** (**theebs**): One of the chief Greek cities.
- **Phikion** (**fi**-kion): The mountain beside Thebes where the Sphinx comes to rest and guard the entrance to the city.

Keyword list

- Tyche's whim.
- The Sphinx.
- The imprisoned people .
- Reward.
- The brothers.
- Parchment.
- Oidipus.
- The riddles.
- Answers.
- The death of the Sphinx.
- King of Thebes.

Synopsis for Winged Words

The people of Thebes are made to suffer for no good reason by the goddess Tyche. She has a Sphinx placed at the city gates, barring entrance to or exit from the city. Anyone who tries must answer the Sphinx's riddles or be consumed by her. No one is able to answer the riddles. Two brothers eventually try to write down the riddles so that they can be worked out. They do not survive but they do manage to write down the riddles. The parchment containing the riddles is blown by the wind to Oidipus who is on his way to Thebes. Using the parchment, and his own wit, he is able to work out the answer to the riddles. He approaches the Sphinx and answers her riddles correctly. She is wounded by his answers and takes herself back to her lair where she devours herself. Oidipus is rewarded by being made king of Thebes. But that is another story ...

Story

Sometimes, and for no reason at all, the gods like to make difficulties for humans, like children playing with toys. When freak events take place and no discernible cause can be identified, such events are attributed by the Greeks to Tyche, goddess of fortune, luck and chance. One day Tyche devised a terrible plan to bring difficulty to the people of Thebes because ... well, for Tyche, there was no 'because'. A Sphinx was summoned to besiege the city and trap its hapless inhabitants. The Sphinx flew towards the city on her enormous wings and came to settle on the side of Mount Phikion which overlooked the road in and out of the city. She was an impressive creature with the lower body of a lion, the wings of a giant eagle and the head and upper body of a beautiful, but vengeful woman.

Whenever somebody tried to enter or leave Thebes, she would glide down from the mountainside, casting a vast shadow over them, and bringing herself to land before them, barring their way into or out of the city. With a voice that whispered, screeched and roared at the same time, she would suggest, demand and declare a riddle. If the unfortunate traveller was unable to answer her riddle successfully then she would lift herself up from the ground with her huge wings and carry him up to her lair on the mountainside where she would first strangle her victim – the word 'sphinx' means 'throttler' – and then she would devour them limb by limb.

The people of Thebes were imprisoned in their own town, and because none who ventured along the road survived, no one knew what the riddle was. Each person who met with the Sphinx had to think about the riddle whilst they stood before the terrifying creature, and they had to think quickly, but none yet had been able to think quickly enough!

At first, some brave citizens ventured forth to confront the Sphinx but as the death count increased, there seemed to be fewer and fewer brave citizens left in the city. The king of Thebes had to begin offering rewards to those willing to try their luck, but the reward had to be increased with each passing day that they remained trapped.

One day, two brothers, between them, found the courage to meet the merciless Sphinx. But they had a plan – a very noble plan. They thought that if they approached her as two, one of them might be able to write down the riddle and perhaps escape back into the city with the riddle written down. Then they would let their wisest citizens pore over the words and solve the puzzle, releasing the people of Thebes from the curse.

The two brothers were never seen nor heard from again, but they had managed to scribble down the riddle on parchment before they met their end. They discovered a terrible surprise that the Sphinx had for her puzzlers, but they managed to warn whoever would find their message of the surprise. As the Sphinx consumed their bodies, the piece of parchment on which the words had been scribbled was blown away from Thebes by the capricious wind.

The wind blew the parchment this way and that, here and there until, at length, it came to rest at the feet of a travelling man called Oidipus. He saw the wind bring him the parchment and so picked it up to see what was written on it. This is what he saw. The parchment, splashed with the blood of the noble brothers, read:

What κρεατυρε has φουρ λεγς ιν θε μορνινγ, two ιν θε αφτερνοον ανδ θρεε ιν θε evening, ανδ θε μορε λεγς ιτ has, θε weaker ιτ ισ;
(a semicolon ';' serves as a question mark '?' in English)

The terrible surprise that the brothers had discovered was that the Sphinx was not asking one riddle but two! *The second one read:*

θερε αρε two σιστερς, ονε gives βιρθ το θε οθερ ανδ she, ιν τυρν, gives βιρθ το θε φιρστ. What αρε they;

Before Oidipus could do anything, he would have to understand what was written on the parchment.

Class Activity: Ancient Greek Workshop

Stop the story here and commence the workshop in Appendix 3. Make sure you are ready with the worksheets for the workshop. Neither Oidipus nor the children can continue until the riddles are understood. Some of the English words have been left in for two reasons: it offers some guidance for the children, and they are words with no direct Ancient Greek equivalent such as 'y' or 'v'.

Story continued …

Now, Oidipus had heard tell of the Sphinx that stood guard at the gates of Thebes, and of the riddle that remained unanswered, and had begun to make his way to the city intent on defeating her. Upon seeing the riddles and the blood, he was able to surmise that this was an ill-fated attempt by someone to write the riddle down. And now it had found its way into his hands, perhaps by the guiding hand of a god or perhaps merely by chance, but nevertheless he now held the key to the city. Oidipus decided to head towards Thebes and to think about the riddles on the way. All he knew was that he must have an answer before he reached the road into the city.

The road into Thebes remained silent and dusty, with not a soul to be seen on this once bustling route. Then, in the distance, the tiny figure of a man appeared, making its way towards the city. It was Oidipus. He drew closer to the city and as he passed the mountainside, just outside the city gates, the sky suddenly darkened. He looked up at the spectacle of the Sphinx as she descended gracefully towards him, silently gliding down to sit before him, her lion's tail curling up as she addressed him with her winged words: 'To pass by me you must first solve this riddle: "What creature has four legs in the morning, two in the afternoon and three in the evening, and the more legs it has, the weaker it is?"'

Oidipus pretended to think about it, then he looked at her and said, 'Well, your words are puzzling indeed, but I think you didn't literally mean in the morning *and* in the afternoon *and* in the evening. *You mean* in the morning of the creature's life. *So the creature you speak of has four legs when an infant, it has two when an adult, and – this one's tricky – it has three legs when old … because it needs a stick to get around. The creature is a* human.'

The Sphinx hissed as the words struck her like a sword to the heart. Then she whispered, screeched and roared, 'You have been lucky and have answered the first of my two riddles, but will Luck be with you for the second or will she abandon you? Now answer the second riddle, if you can!' Then she delivered the second riddle with a faint but unpleasant smile: 'There are two sisters: one gives birth to the other and she, in turn, gives birth to the first. What are they?'

Oidipus feigned deep thought again and then said, almost as if to himself, 'Well, when I realised that you didn't literally mean 'in the morning' in the first riddle, I wonder if the same trick is being used in the second. At first it seems impossible: how can two sisters also be each other's mothers? But last night, I could not sleep so I lay and looked up to the sky as day turned into night, and I lay all night looking up to the stars until night then turned into day. It's as if day gives birth to night and then it's as if night gives birth to day in an endless cycle of motherhood. Yet they stand next to each other like sisters locked in an eternal dance. Could it be that the sisters are … night and day?

The Sphinx hissed at him: 'You speak as though you have had time to think about my words. How could you have known the riddles as you lay and looked at the stars for assistance?'

Oidipus held up the parchment and said, 'I have struck you in the heart but not with a sword; I have wounded you with winged words instead, brought to me on the wind like a death spell for you. It was with words that you hoped to entrap me and it is with words that I have defeated you.'

She screeched like a dying animal and lifted herself up into the air with giant movements of her wings. She took herself to her lair, and, just as she had devoured the unhappy men who had failed to answer her riddles, paradoxically, akin to the sisters night *and* day, *she devoured herself. She was finally free from her vengefulness, free from the whimsical commands of the gods and free from having to strangle the hapless inhabitants of Thebes. Her screeching and her riddles vanished forever.*

Oidipus strode through the gates of Thebes, the emaciated people of which looked at him disbelieving as they witnessed the first person to enter their city in a long time. By now, and out of desperation, the reward was for no less than the throne of Thebes itself. The adventure, however, was far from over for Oidipus.

The true riddle of the Sphinx put to the people of Thebes had remained unanswered, however, even with the death of the Sphinx. It was this: 'Why? And why us?'

Destiny, fate and chance

TQ: Why do bad things happen?

Nested Questions

- Do things happen for a reason?
- Why do the gods make things difficult for the characters in the myths?
- Can bad things that happen be good for us in any way?
- Why don't the gods just make good things happen?

Bibliography and Recommended Reading

Books

Goldhill, Simon (2005). *Love, Sex and Tragedy, Why Classics Matters*. John Murray Publishers Ltd.

Grimm J. L and W. C. (1909). *Grimm's Fairy Tales*. Trans. Mrs Edgar Lucas. 9th edn 2002. Constable & Co.

Homer (1991). *The Odyssey*. Trans. E. V. Rieu. Revised D. C. H. Rieu. Introduction by Peter Jones. Penguin Classics.

Jones, Peter (2004). *Learn Ancient Greek*. Duckworth.

Lupton, Hugh, Morden, Daniel and Balit, Christina (2010). *The Adventures of Odysseus*. Barefoot Books.

MacIntyre, A. (1981). *After Virtue*. Duckworth.

March, Jenny (1998). *Dictionary of Classical Mythology*. Cassell.

Thomas, Taffy and Killick, Steve (2007). *Telling Tales: Storytelling as Emotional Literacy*. Educational Printing Services.

Williams, Bernard (2007). *Life as Narrative*. Blackwell Publishing.

Worley, Peter (2011). *The If Machine: Philosophical Enquiry in the Classroom*. Continuum.

Online Resources

The *Iliad* of Homer, translated by Herbert Jordan: http://www.iliadtranslation. com/winged_words.html

Online Etymology Dictionary: http://www.etymonline.com/index.php

Perseus online resource: http://www.perseus.tufts.edu/hopper/

The Philosophy Foundation, for more philosophy sessions, training and philosophers in schools: www.philosophy-foundation.org

Standford Encycleopaedia of Philosophy: http://plato.stanford.edu/